Understanding

the
Trinity

Max Hatton

Understanding the Trinity
Copyright © 2001 Max Hatton

All rights reserved. No part of this publication may be reproduced
in any form without prior permission from the publisher.

British Library Cataloguing in Publication Data.
A catalogue record for this book is available
from the British Library.

All Bible quotations are taken from the New International
Version unless stated otherwise.

ISBN 1-873796-93-5

First published 2001
AUTUMN HOUSE
Alma Park Grantham.
Lincs., England.
NG31 9SL

10 9 8 7 6 5 4 3 2

Dedication

Dedicated to my dear wife Merle.
A minister can have no greater asset than a
loving wife who is also dedicated to God.
Merle has been a wife such as this.
She has been the greatest asset I have had in my ministry.
We both thank our most gracious, loving God for bringing
us out of darkness into His wonderful light.

Appreciation

A note of heartfelt appreciation is offered to our dear friends Geoff Rogerson (a Christian from Denmark, Western Australia), and Pastor Austin G. Fletcher (now of Cooranbong, New South Wales). Geoff helped us out of the darkness of the Watchtower influence some thirty years ago, and Austin helped us into the light of Christianity.

I will always be indebted also to two special friends – Ted Chambers (deceased) and Jock Ainsworth also of Western Australia. These two men helped with the expenses of our move from Western Australia (my wife and I and four children) to Cooranbong, New South Wales. They also assisted in the payment of college fees. God put it into their hearts to help us. If He had not done this I would never have been able to study for the ministry. Their generosity towards us was appreciated enormously. May their spiritual tribe increase.

We thank our gracious God for the great love which He distributes through the hands of His wonderful people.

Prepared at 'The Little Palace',
Unit 51, Kressville Units,
Cooranbong, NSW, 2265.
© 2001.

Contents

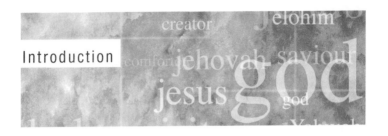

The author first encounters the Trinity doctrine

have long held a special interest in this subject. At one time, I regret to say, I was antagonistic to the concept and also to all who believed it to be true. Although I was christened as a Methodist and attended Sunday School as a boy, (even topping the State of Western Australia in the Scripture examination of the Young People's department in 1945), I was really ignorant of the teachings of the Bible and turned my back on God and the Church when I became 'a wise man of the world' – at about the age of 15! In fact, I did all the wrong things from God's point of view and indulged in smoking, drinking alcohol, gambling, and such like.

From a little time before I married my precious wife Merle in 1954, I began to modify my habits considerably. At the time of our marriage I was working in a local government office in a suburb of Perth, Western Australia. Eventually, I advanced to the position of Shire Clerk. It was in this capacity that I became involved with Jehovah's Witnesses. My assistant shire clerk, unbeknown to me at first, had recently become a follower of the Watchtower

Society. Because of our friendship we got to studying the subject of christening because my wife and I intended to have our son christened in the Methodist Church. We had already taken this step with our eldest child. This led to discussion on other subjects and, because of my very limited knowledge of the Bible, I, with my wife, eventually accepted Watchtower teaching and were baptized on 14 November 1959.

Most of what followed must be the subject of another paper, but I will state here that I learned all the Watchtower objections to the Trinity teaching and I became a vigorous campaigner against the Trinity. After a few years of association with the Watchtower followers, I came to realize that much of what they teach is quite out of harmony with the Bible. On 16 August 1964, I resigned from Jehovah's Witnesses and never attended any more of their meetings. The Watchtower Society uses disfellowshipping as a device to silence those who sever their relationship with them. They realize that such people can expose many of their falsehoods so Jehovah's Witnesses are forbidden to associate with people who leave the organization. They cannot discuss their beliefs with even their closest relatives who leave. The close relatives who remain are disfellowshiped if they have spiritual association of any sort with a loved one who has left. As a consequence, even though I had resigned about nine months previously, I was formally advised that I had been disfellowshipped on 1 July 1965. This was an amazing sequence of events. I resigned and began to believe and teach other than what the Watchtower Society teaches. Even though I had resigned nine months prior to this, they disfellowshipped me because they said I was following an *'apostate course'*. An unbelievable situation? You would think so, but it is true nevertheless. Are all other people who are not Jehovah's Witnesses following an apostate course? Hardly! Could they be disfellowshipped even though they are not Jehovah's Witnesses? Such a suggestion sounds quite ridiculous, and it is. But the lengths the Watchtower followers are bidden to go to silence former members is also ridiculous.

When we gave up following the Watchtower Society, my wife and I decided that we would not give up our faith in God or in the Bible. It became clear to us that we had made the mistake other Jehovah's Witnesses make of following men. We accepted that we were the ones who had been wrong, not God. But we were really in a wilderness state; we felt unable to fellowship with other Christian groups because of the Trinity doctrine. This doctrine loomed in front of us like a huge mountain. I spent more than a year studying the subject and eventually had to admit defeat. I found that the Trinity doctrine is a doctrine of Scripture and I have maintained a continuing interest in it ever since. In fact, while attending Avondale College, New South Wales, Australia, to prepare for the ministry, I wrote my major essay for the theological course on this subject.

Over the years I have been interested to note that those who deviate from the truth on the subject, or in other ways oppose it, don't really understand what they are opposing. When we take into account all that the Bible teaches about God we find ourselves compelled to accept that while there is only one true God by nature, the Bible insists that the Father is God, that Jesus is God, and that the Holy Spirit is God. Bible-believing Christians are, therefore, compelled to accept that God is a Tri-unity.

All Bible quotations are taken from the New International Version unless stated otherwise.

Chapter 1

An introduction to the doctrine of the Trinity

A natural reaction to the title of my essay, *Understanding the Trinity*, might sometimes be, 'What impertinence even to suggest that the infinite God can be understood.' It is true that God is far beyond our comprehension. We must not fall into the trap of thinking we can absolutely define the indefinable or fully comprehend the incomprehensible. God is a Being who is in every way infinite. Only the Infinite can possibly understand the infinite. When we try to understand some things about God we go crashing against the ceilings of our minds. It is clear that if we could fully understand the nature of God, He would no longer be God. God is the only Being for whom no mysteries exist. How thankful we ought to be, though, for the truth expressed by Martin Luther:

God is incomprehensible, but He is not unknowable.

We can know God personally and we can know some things about His nature. Be assured, though, that these things can only be properly understood through divine revelation. What God has chosen to reveal to us should be cherished by us and should be the subject of our diligent study. The principle found in **Deuteronomy 29:29** should be applied in this, and for that matter, in all biblical study:

'The secret things belong to the LORD our God, but the things revealed belong to us and to our children.'

'The things revealed.' The things God has revealed about Himself are for our study. Our study leads those of us who are Christians to assert that God is a Triunity. Read on and the reasons for this will become clear to you.

First of all, what do Christians mean by this doctrine? My initial intention is to provide what has been an accepted formula for the doctrine, and then to reveal why such a formula is required by Scripture. I will then further elaborate on the concept of the Trinity. Often-raised objections will be dealt with along the way.

Basic scriptural facts requiring us to accept that God is a Trinity

There are two basic facts taught in Scripture which require us to conclude that God is a Trinity:

- There is only one true God.
- The Father, the Son, and the Holy Spirit are all revealed to be God but separate Persons.

If we are to be faithful to Scripture we are required to teach that the one God comprises three Persons. Early Christians seem to have been content to accept these facts and to let it go at that. It was only as dissenters sought to deviate from these biblical basics that it became necessary to attempt an explanation of the interrelationship of the Three.

An early Christian attempt to explain the Trinity

The Trinitarian formulas were established in the midst of considerable controversy stretching over several centuries.

One of the most notable of these ancient statements is the Athanasian Creed. A modern translation by Roger Beckwith, of appropriate portions of the Creed, follows:

Whosoever wishes to be saved

Before all things it is necessary that he hold the catholic faith, which faith, if anyone does not keep it whole and unharmed, without doubt he will perish everlastingly.

Now, the catholic faith is this, that we worship one God in Trinity, and Trinity in Unity, neither confusing the Persons nor dividing the divine Being.

For there is one Person of the Father, another of the Son, and another of the Holy Spirit, but the Godhead of the Father, the Son and the Holy Spirit is all one, their glory equal, their majesty co-eternal.

Such as the Father is, such is the Son and such is the Holy Spirit: the Father uncreated, the Son uncreated and the Holy Spirit uncreated, the Father infinite, the Son infinite and the Holy Spirit infinite, the Father eternal, the Son eternal and the Holy Spirit eternal; and yet they are not three Eternals but one Eternal, just as they are not three Uncreateds, nor three Infinites, but one Uncreated and one Infinite.

In the same way, the Father is almighty, the Son almighty and the Holy Spirit almighty, and yet they are not three Almighties but one Almighty.

Thus, the Father is God, the Son is God and the Holy Spirit is God, and yet there are not three Gods but one God.

Thus, the Father is the Lord, the Son is the Lord and the Holy Spirit is the Lord, and yet not three Lords but one Lord.

Because, just as we are compelled by Christian

truth to confess each Person singly to be both God and Lord, so we are forbidden by the catholic religion to say, There are three Gods, or three Lords.

The Father is from none, not made nor created nor begotten; the Son is from the Father alone, not made nor created, but begotten; the Holy Spirit is from the Father and the Son, not made nor created nor begotten, but proceeding.

So there is one Father, not three Fathers; one Son, not three Sons; one Holy Spirit, not three Holy Spirits.

And in this Trinity there is no before or after, no greater or less, but all three Persons are co-eternal with each other and co-equal.

So that in all things, as has already been said, the Trinity in Unity, and Unity in Trinity, is to be worshipped.

He therefore who wishes to be saved let him think thus of the Trinity.[1]

This formula has served Christians well for about two millennia. I would, however, make two observations with reference to it:

● The word 'catholic' means 'universal' and is not a reference to the Roman Catholic Church.

● The assertion that the Son is 'begotten' would hardly be included if the statement was made today. The reasons for this will become apparent in future pages.

Examples of Trinity-type statements of early Christians

The fact that early Christians held a Trinitarian belief is evident from the writings of many of the Church Fathers. This is documented in many publications. They had not yet felt it necessary to formulate a sophisticated statement of the implications of their belief and, unfortunately, this allowed many unacceptable ideas to develop. The Arian heresy was one that flourished. So Christians were compelled to get together and clarify what Scripture required them to accept as a legitimate doctrine clarifying the complexity of God.

The following are but a few examples of the many statements made by the early Church Fathers:

Clement of Rome, who lived at the end of the first century, wrote:
For as God lives, and the Lord Jesus Christ lives, and the holy Spirit, who are the faith and hope of God's chosen.

Ignatius, also from the end of the first century, wrote to the Magnesians and commenced a sentence:
The apostles did to the Father and to Christ and the Spirit . . . .

In *The Martyrdom of Polycarp* (AD70-156) we read:
The Lord Jesus Christ gather me also with his chosen into his heavenly kingdom! To him be glory with the Father and the holy Spirit forever and ever. Amen.

R. A. Finlayson reveals the true situation:
There is the fact that when the doctrine of the Trinity in Unity came to be formulated, it was immediately accepted as an expression of what had been the faith of the Church from the beginning. One thing is clear, that the doctrine of the Trinity was not arrived at as a result of philosophic reasoning, but was due entirely to

meditation on the facts of revelation given in the Scriptures of both the Old Testament and the New, and more especially on the facts concerning the Person of Christ, and God's relation to the world of men through His Spirit.[2]

An explanation of a theologian of today

Millard J. Erickson provides a worthwhile summary of what we can understand of the Trinity:

The Trinity is a communion of three persons, three centers of consciousness, who exist and always have existed in union with one another and in dependence on one another. Each is dependent for his life on each of the others. They share their lives, having such a close relationship that each is conscious of what the other is conscious of. They have never had any prior independent existence, and will not and cannot have any such now or in the future. Each is essential to the life of each of the others, and to the life of the Trinity. They are bound to one another in love, agape love, which therefore unites them in the closest and most intimate of relationships. This unselfish, agape love makes each more concerned for the other than for himself. There is therefore a mutual submission of each to each of the others and a mutual glorifying of one another. There is complete equality of the three. There has been, to be sure, temporary subordination of one member of the Trinity to the other, but this is functional rather than essential. At the same time, this unity and equality do not require identity of function. There are certain roles that distinctively belong primarily to one, although all participate in the function of each.[3]

The complexity of God is to be expected

We must remember, as we think these matters through, that we are travelling down a pathway of discovery which is not entirely clear to us. As C. S. Lewis said when he was discussing this subject:

> If Christianity was something we were making up, of course we could make it easier, but it is not. We cannot compete, in simplicity, with people who are inventing religions. How could we? We are dealing with fact. Of course anyone can be simple if he has no facts to bother about.[4]

I have read comments on the Athanasian Creed which try to ridicule it and make out that it is a mass of confusion. It is only confusing to those who don't want to understand it. Trinitarians do not find it at all confusing. We do our Maker no compliment by trying to represent Him as simple to understand. Please explore this aspect of our study with me.

The story is told of St Augustine, who was walking along the beach one day considering the complexity of the doctrine of the Trinity. So engrossed in thought was he that he almost stumbled upon a child playing on the seashore. The child had dug a hole above the waterline and was shovelling water from the ocean into the hole.

'What are you doing?' queried Augustine.

'I am shovelling all the water from the ocean into this hole,' replied the child.

'Come on now,' responded Augustine, 'you cannot hope to fit all the water from that vast ocean into that small hole!'

'And neither can you understand all about the infinite God in that small mind of yours,' exclaimed the child. Augustine continued his walk feeling quite stunned and later stated that he must have met an angel.

In an endeavour to try to simplify the teaching some have suggested various illustrations. For example, water can exist as a solid, a liquid, or a gas. John Wesley was once challenged by a sceptic to prove the doctrine of the Trinity. Wesley asked to be excused for a moment and came back with three lighted candles. *'Here are three lights,'* He said, *'but there is only one light, you explain this to me, and I will explain to you the doctrine of the Trinity.'* There was only one light, but in reality there were three and these two facts existed at the same time. Three lights merged into one. This is probably the best illustration I have encountered. However, there are really no analogies. God is unique. There is really nothing with which we can compare Him. Things which are temporal and have spatial elements cannot possibly illustrate the eternal God who is infinite. In fact, Isaiah insisted that this was so millennia ago by asking rhetorical questions:

> *'To whom, then, will you compare God? What image will you compare him to?'* **Isaiah 40:18.**

Of course there are many things we accept which we don't understand. How could everything be created out of nothing? I don't know, but I nevertheless am a committed creationist. How could Jesus be born of a virgin? I don't know, but I believe in the virgin birth because God revealed this truth to me in His word. I don't understand what light is and I don't believe that anyone else does either. Some say it is made of particles while others suggest it is composed of waves. There are those who say it consists of a combination of the two. I believe in light even though I do not understand it!

It may help us to appreciate the complexity of God by

comparing ourselves to a unicellular amoeba. An amoeba is a microscopic form of life consisting of a single cell. Humans are vastly more complex for we consist of millions of cells. It is plain to see that as we go up the scale of creatures the more complex the organism becomes. If the gap between an amoeba and ourselves is vast, and it is, surely we would expect nothing less than that the gap between ourselves and God would be enormously greater. We would expect God to be of a complexity far beyond our understanding. When we try to understand God we are like people standing on the shore of a mighty ocean – beholding its vastness but understanding it to only a small degree. Informed Christians will humbly admit that they cannot fully explain God.

The problem of trying to describe God in human language

Misunderstanding is sometimes caused by not appreciating the problem that follows. We must realize that human language is quite inadequate to describe God.

Human languages have developed so that humans can describe things they observe and talk about their experiences. Therefore, human language is only really adequate to describe things on the human level. We must acknowledge that we are incapable of seeing, knowing, or experiencing the completeness of God. We simply don't have words adequate to describe Him. When we use the word 'person' we are prone to think of persons of the type we know. When we think of the three persons of the Trinity we are likely to think of them as we would three human persons. That is three persons of the **same sort of substance (essence)**. But, because there is only One God, the three persons must be of the **same substance (essence)**. Three human persons would be **exclusive** – independent of one another. The three persons of the Trinity, however, must be **inclusive** and not independent of one another. Because there is but one true God, by nature we have to conclude that He is plural as to persons but single as to **substance.** Human language is inadequate, but it is the only vehicle we have to talk about God. To paraphrase Augustine:

We use the word 'persons', not because we want to use it, but because otherwise we would be reduced to silence.

The use of summary terminology

The summary title given to this Bible truth is 'The Trinity'. There is no valid reason to claim that the doctrine cannot be true because the word 'Trinity' does not appear in the Bible. Many other words describing Bible truth do not occur in it either. Examples are 'millennium', 'theocracy', 'Incarnation', and 'eschatology'. Such terminology is helpful in that it allows much to be said by the use of a single word. In what follows it will become very clear why I have accepted that the Father, Jesus, and the Holy Spirit are all part of the one true God.

I am trying, to the best of my ability to be as simple as possible in my comments and explanations. However, we are delving into a complicated subject which can be clarified considerably but this, nevertheless, will require a diligent effort on the part of my readers if they are to avail themselves of the full value of my work. The Bible, said William Barclay, is like a large pool. It has shallows in which a little lamb can wade but there are also great depths in which even an elephant could swim. May I repeat that our desire to understand what we can of God involves us in the study of a very complicated subject which surely requires of us a commitment to immerse ourselves in the very depths of the Word of God.

We have seen what the Trinity teaching is. We now need to move into the Bible itself, Old Testament and New Testament, in order to satisfy ourselves whether Christians are correct in claiming that the Bible teaches that God is a Trinity. If Christians are correct, we will expect to find evidence that the Father is God, evidence that teaches that Jesus, the Son, is God, and evidence revealing that the Holy Spirit is a separate Person, and that He too is God. In addition, we will anticipate finding clear references indicating that there is only One True God by nature.

It is my pleasure then to invite you to come on a journey of discovery with me as we move into a study of the Bible teaching on the basics which require our belief in the Trinity. We will seek to understand what God has revealed of Himself.

---

[1] Gerald Bray, *Creeds, Councils and Christ,* Inter Varsity Press, Leicester, England, 1984, pages 209, 210.

[2] R. A. Finlayson, *The Story of Theology,* The Tyndale Press, London, 1963, page 14.

[3] Millard J. Erickson, *God in Three Persons,* Baker Books, Grand Rapids, Michigan, 1995, page 331.

[4] C. S. Lewis, *Mere Christianity,* Collins, Fontana Books, London, 1964, pages 140, 141.

Chapter 2

There is but one true God by nature

S cripture opens with the assumption that the existence of God is so self evident that proof of this fact is unnecessary. The opening statement is simple and direct, *'In the beginning God . . .'*

One of the greatest facts of human history, though one that is not usually appreciated today, is that God has communicated with us, He has revealed things about Himself to us, and made us aware of His purpose in creating us, in the pages of the Holy Bible.

The Bible makes it abundantly clear that there is only one true God. He is the Creator. Others are offered the title God in a secondary sense in that they are acting on the part of God exercising His prerogatives. As might be expected there are also subversive imposters who seek to usurp the place of God. These too are regarded as God by deluded people.

There is but one true God:

Here are a few examples confirming this Scriptural fact:

Deuteronomy 4:35 *the LORD is God; besides him there is no other.*

Deuteronomy 4:39 *the LORD is God in heaven above and on the earth below. There is no other.*

Deuteronomy 32:39 *See now that I myself am He! There is no god besides me.*

1 Kings 8:60 *the LORD is God and that there is no other.*

Isaiah 44:6 *I am the first and I am the last; apart from me there is no God.*

Isaiah 45:5 *I am the LORD, and there is no other; apart from me there is no God.*

James 2:19 *You believe that there is one God. Good! Even the demons believe that – and shudder.*

Some, acting on behalf of God, are called 'God'

Exodus 6:28-7:1 *Now when the LORD spoke to Moses in Egypt, he said to him, 'I am the LORD. Tell Pharaoh king of Egypt everything I tell you.' But Moses said to the LORD, 'Since I speak with faltering lips, why would Pharaoh listen to me?' Then the LORD said to Moses, 'See, I have made you like God to Pharoah, and your brother Aaron will be your prophet.'*

Psalm 82:1 *God presides in the great assembly; he gives judgment among the 'gods'.*

God calls the unjust Judges 'gods'. They were supposed to be acting upon His authority but in reality were going about things in their own way. For this reason some suggest that they are being called 'gods' in an ironic sense. They had made themselves the supreme authority. They were no longer acting on behalf of God but had, as it were, made themselves gods. It is evident that they were not God by nature; they were not true God.

There are false gods

2 Corinthians 4:4 describes the devil as *'The god of this age'.* He too is not true God.

Galatians 4:8 makes the point that false gods are not god by nature: *Formerly, when you did not know God, you were slaves to those who by nature are not gods.*

Acts 19:26 reports the teaching of the apostle Paul: *He says that man-made gods are no gods at all.*

1 Corinthians 10:20 Paul says that false gods are demons: *The sacrifices of pagans are offered to demons, not to God.*

The Scriptures cited are only a sampling of what could be offered. The point that there is only one true God by nature is beyond dispute. Others referred to as god are either acting on behalf of God, exercising His prerogatives, or are false gods.

As a young man I had no interest in God because I understood Him to be an angry God who roasted people eternally in fiery flames. I rejected Him without really understanding who or what He was. I later discovered that

God had received bad press; He is not at all as I had understood Him to be, in fact I came to the understanding that He is quite the opposite. I discovered that the basic attitude of God is not anger, or vengeance seeking, but love; *1 John 4:8.*

God is love!

This fact should be advertised constantly, through every media outlet, all over the world. It should be shouted from the highest mountains. God's every thought, His every intention, His every action is permeated with perfect love. **1 Peter 5:7** admonishes us to: *Cast all your anxiety on him because he cares for you.*

> **1 John 4:7** *love comes from God.*

> **1 John 4:16** *we know and rely on the love God has for us.*

How precious are the words that form what has been regarded as the best known verse in the Bible:

> **John 3:16** *'For God so loved the world that he gave his one and only Son, that whoever believes in him shall not perish but have eternal life.'*

> **Romans 5:8** *God demonstrates his own love for us in this: While we were still sinners, Christ died for us.*

A profile of some other basic attributes of God

Psalm 139:7-12 Omnipresence – God is everywhere present
Psalm 139:1-4 Omniscience – God knows all things
Matthew 19:26 Omnipotence – God is all powerful
Psalm 90:2 Eternal – God has always been there

Malachi 3:6 Immutable – God never changes
Psalm 145:9 Goodness – God is good
Psalm 19:7-9 Righteousness – God is righteous, holy

While there is but one true God, and we have but touched upon the wonders concerning Him, Inspiration has made it abundantly clear that there is a plurality within the substance of God. This was made evident to God's people right from the beginning. Would we dare deny the evidence of Scripture?

Evidences of plurality in God in the Old Testament are hints of the Trinity

Evidence of plurality in God is often found in passages throughout the Old Testament. These must surely be seen as hints of the triune nature of God revealed more clearly in the New Testament.

The very first verse of the Bible begins by describing God with the plural name Elohim – *'In the beginning God (Elohim).'* If God is just a solitary Being we would not expect to find Him speaking of Himself in the plural. On the other hand, if He is a plurality of Persons we would expect to find Him doing this.

In fact, plural and singular references to God and Lord occur frequently in the Bible. In ***Genesis 1:26, 27*** we find God saying, *'Let us make man in our image, in our likeness* ***(plural)*** *. . . . So God created man in his own likeness'* ***(singular)***.

*Genesis 3:22 The man has now become like **one of us**.*

*Genesis 11:7, 8 Let **us** go down and confuse their language. . . . So the LORD scattered them.*

Isaiah 6:8 *Then I heard the voice of the LORD saying, 'Whom shall I send? And who will go for **us**?'*

The plural and singular references are obvious. Some who oppose the Trinity teaching try to dismiss the examples given as being the plural of majesty. Wasn't it Queen Victoria who exclaimed, 'We are not amused!'? It is up to the opposers to provide evidence that such a usage existed in the Hebrew language. As G. A. F. Knight says:

Surely that is to read into Hebrew speech a modern way of thinking. The kings of Israel and Judah are all addressed in the singular in our biblical records.[1]

Robert Morey provides a very interesting account of how this excuse for denying the value of the plural references to God came to be:

*During the nineteenth century debates between Unitarians and Trinitarians, the principle of **pluralis majestaticus** was revealed to be a hoax popularized by the famous Jewish scholar Gesenius. It became clear that he used it as a **ruse de guerre** against Christianity.*

The fundamental error resided in the attempt to take a modern monarchical idiosyncrasy and read it back into an ancient text when such an idiosyncrasy was unknown at that time. Richard Davies in 1891 pointed out, 'Indeed, this royal style is unknown in Scripture.'

What is astounding is that, one hundred years later, the anti-Trinitarians are still using this hoax to dodge the significance of the use of plural pronouns in reference to God. They seem to be totally ignorant of the fact that it is a recent grammatical invention and, thus, cannot be read back into ancient times or texts.[2]

A couple of other more than a little interesting references to the plurality in God follow:

> **Zechariah 3:2** *The LORD said to Satan, 'The LORD rebuke you, Satan!'* (We have one who is named Yahweh requesting Yahweh to rebuke Satan).

We again encounter two persons having the name Yahweh:

> **Genesis 19:24** *Then the LORD rained down burning sulphur on Sodom and Gomorrah – from the LORD out of the heavens.*

There is an unmistakable plurality in these references to God. On the other hand the **Shema**, the Jewish statement of faith, reveals the oneness of God quite clearly. It is found in **Deuteronomy 6:4, 5:**

> *Hear, O Israel: The LORD our God, the LORD is one.*

The important point about this statement, often over-looked, is that the word 'one' is *echad* and this does not deny the possibility of plurality within the oneness. If Moses had wanted to use a word that does require a strict solitariness he would have used the word *yachid*. Please consider the comments of Graeme Goldsworthy:

> *Here, as we find it consistently throughout the Old Testament, God is proclaimed as one (Hebrew:* **echad***). The nature of God's oneness must be understood from the revelation of the whole Bible, but this word* **one** *does not rule out a complexity or plurality within the oneness. Thus, the same word is used of husband and wife becoming one flesh (Genesis 2:24), of Pharaoh's two dreams being one (Genesis 41:25), and of a nation gathering, as one man (Judges 20:1).*[3]

In the light of our brief survey of hints of the Trinity in the Old Testament we must acknowledge that the doctrine was there in seed form but it found a much clearer expression in the New Testament. This is, of course, the case with many things for, as has often been said, 'What is latent in the Old Testament becomes patent in the New Testament.'

[1] G. A. F. Knight, *A Biblical Approach to the Doctrine of the Trinity* (Scottish Journal of Theology, Occasional Papers No. 1) Oliver and Boyd, Edinburgh, 1953, page 20.

[2] Robert Morey, *THE TRINITY Evidence and Issues*, World Publishing, Grand Rapids, Michigan, 1996, page 95.

[3] Graeme Goldsworthy, *Gospel and Wisdom*, Paternoster Press, Carlisle, UK, 1995, page 161.

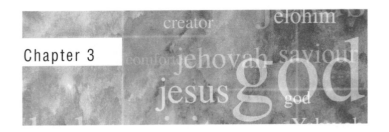

Chapter 3

The Father and the Son are God

When Jesus came upon the scene of human history the understanding of God by believers began to change quite dramatically. It was as though the light God had for man during the time of the plan of redemption was controlled by a dimmer switch. When Jesus came to live among us, God turned it up to full power. The understanding that believers had of God was greatly illuminated and they came gradually to comprehend a much clearer picture of the complexity of the one true God.

As we read the New Testament we recognize that there was an awakening consciousness among Christians of the deity of Jesus. Inspiration caused them to acknowledge this here and there in the sacred writings. They nevertheless clearly recognized that God was still in heaven but He was, at the same time, present with them here on Earth in the Person of Jesus Christ.

The Fatherhood of God

In Old Testament times God is most often identified by names He applied to Himself through inspired writers. He is sometimes referred to as Elohim (God) but His most prominent name was Yahweh. The divine name Yahweh is used more than 6,800 times in the Old Testament, sometimes in combination with other words. An example is 'Yahweh Tsidkenu', which means 'Yahweh our righteousness'.

While the primary way God is referred to in the Old Testament is by means of the name Yahweh, He is sometimes described in ways that are familiar to humans in order that we may appreciate various of His characteristics. We can only think of Him in terms of analogies, so He is sometimes pictured as such things as a Judge, a King, or a rock. *Deuteronomy 32:18* would encourage us to think of Him as both Father and Mother.

Similarly, Yahweh is identified as a Father on a few occasions in the Old Testament. The term was used to signify the special relationship He had with His people Israel as the Creator of the Nation (*Deuteronomy 32:6; Jeremiah 31:9*). It was also used of the special relationship He had with the Messianic line, the seed of David (*2 Samuel 7:14; 1 Chronicles 22:10; Psalm 2:7*).

'Father' in the New Testament

While God was known in Old Testament times by the name Yahweh, this name does not appear in the New Testament Greek manuscripts, because Yahweh is Hebrew. Yahweh is translated in the Septuagint (the Greek Old Testament) as 'Kupios'. 'Kupios' is used in the New Testament several times; *Acts 18:8-9,* for example. See the quotation from Howard Marshall on pages 82, 83.

There, in the light of progressive revelation, God is revealed as a Trinity – Father, Son, and Holy Spirit. See on this the statement by Benjamin Warfield in chapter 13.

Old Testament people, in Covenant relationship with God, were not taught that the way to address God was by calling Him Father. However, when Jesus came along He taught His disciples that to address God as Father was *the* way. Consequently, God is called Father more than 165 times in the four gospels, while Paul calls Him Father over forty times. The most prominent instruction given by Jesus on this matter is no doubt that found in what is commonly called the Lord's Prayer:

Matthew 6:9 *This is how you should pray: 'Our Father in heaven . . .'*

So we see that God, in relationship with His spiritual children, is to be called Father.

1 John 3:1 *How great is the love the Father has lavished on us, that we should be called children of God!*

Matthew 23:9 *And do not call anyone on earth 'father,' for you have one Father, and he is in heaven.*

A general survey of sonship in the Bible

While all Christians recognize God as their Father and that they, by adoption, are His children, or sons, the Sonship of Jesus is on an entirely different level. It would be most helpful for us to consider the question of Sonship next.

The book *The Christadelphian Instructor,* by Robert Roberts, (Logos Publications, Box 220, Findon, South Australia 5023, no date) says on page 17: *Co-eternity is impossible in a son.*

Such uninformed statements could never be made if the following advice was understood and heeded:

We cannot build up our doctrines, or compile our

theology, simply by repeating the biblical statements without regard for the meaning of the terms then and now. We have the added responsibility of re-expressing the statements so that their original meaning is clear to people today.[1]

Informed Bible students know that 'son of God' is used in at least four different ways in Scripture. George Eldon Ladd provides a very helpful discussion on this subject. The following are the headings under which he discusses this term.[2] The comments are my own:

- **The nativistic sense:**

This applies to those who owe their existence to the immediate creative activity of God.

> ***Luke 3:38*** *Adam, the son of God.*

> ***Exodus 4:22, 23*** *'This is what the LORD says: Israel is my firstborn son.'*

> ***Luke 1:35*** *The angel answered, 'The Holy Spirit will come upon you, and the power of the Most High will overshadow you. So the holy one to be born will be called the Son of God.'*

- **The moral-religious sense:**

God regards those who are in a special loving relationship with Him as His children – ***John 1:12; Matthew 5:45; 1 John 3:1***. He adopts us as His children – ***Romans 8:14, 19; Galatians 3:26; 4:5***.

- **The messianic sense:**

The Davidic king is designated the son of God – ***2 Samuel 7:14; Psalm 2:6, 7; 89:26, 27***.

- **The theological sense:**

Jesus is the Son of God *(Hebrews 4:14)* in a different way from all of these. While Christians are sons of God, Jesus is *the* Son of God. We will explore this matter now but I must emphasize first of all that Scripture does not necessarily use the term in its modern-day literal sense. We must never overlook the fact that the Bible is a book of an Eastern culture written about 2,000 to 3,500 years ago. It is imperative that we study it and let it speak to us in order for us to ascertain a true understanding of the terminology it uses.

Jesus is the Son of God but His Sonship is unshared

The Sonship of Jesus is shown by Inspiration to be different from that of the others mentioned above. In *Matthew 11:27* (compare *Luke 10:22*), Jesus claimed that He alone knows the Father fully:

Matthew 11:27 '*All things have been committed to me by my Father. No-one knows the Son except the Father, and no-one knows the Father except the Son and those to whom the Son chooses to reveal him.*'

Jesus became the Son of God at His human birth as mentioned under the first point above. However, He was the Son of God in a completely different way as well. His relationship with the Father is exclusive. It is an undeniable fact that Jesus went out of His way to avoid placing Himself on the same level as others in their relationship to the Father. He was careful not to embrace others by saying *'Our Father'* when referring to God. In *Matthew 5:16, 45* He refers to God as *'Your Father'* – *see also Luke 12:30*. So careful was Jesus to maintain this stance that at *John 20:17* He advised His followers, '*I am returning to my*

Father and your Father, to my God and your God.'

It is true that when Jesus gave to His followers His 'Model Prayer' (The Lord's Prayer); He taught them to pray 'Our Father'. However, we need to note carefully that He was not praying then; He was simply offering to them a style of prayer for them to follow.

The unshared Sonship of Jesus

There are passages in the New Testament which clearly require us to accept that the Sonship of Jesus indicates His 'likeness' and 'sameness of nature' with the Father. Lorraine Boettner provides a statement, representative of those of many others, which supports the truthfulness of my claim:

> *In connection with an earlier treatment of the doctrine of the Trinity we have pointed out that in theological language the terms 'Father' and 'Son' carry with them not our occidental ideas of, on the one hand, source of being and superiority, and on the other, subordination and dependence, but rather the Semitic and oriental ideas of* **likeness** *or* **sameness of nature** *and equality of being. It is, of course, the Semitic consciousness that underlies the phraseology of Scripture and wherever the Scriptures call Christ the 'Son of God' they assert His true and proper Deity. It signifies a unique relationship that cannot be predicated of nor shared with any creature. As any merely human son is like his father in his essential nature, that is, possessed of humanity, so Christ, the Son of God, was like His Father in His essential nature, that is, possessed of Deity.*[3]

It is not at all difficult to find confirmation of the word 'Son', or similar, being used to indicate identification.

35

Please note the following references:

1 Kings 20:35 *'sons of the prophets'* meant 'of the order of the prophets'.

Mark 3:17 *'Sons of Thunder'* is used of James and John because of their fiery nature.

Matthew 13:38 Christians are called *'sons of the kingdom'*, while the wicked are termed *'sons of the evil one'*.

John 8:44 Jesus condemned some Jews, advising them, *'You belong to your father, the devil.'*

1 Thessalonians 5:5 Paul spoke to some Christians, advising, *'you are all sons of light and sons of the day. We do not belong to the night or to the darkness.'*

JOHN 5:17 *'My Father is always at work to this very day, and I, too, am working.'*

Here Jesus is acknowledging that His Sonship places Him in equality with God. The claim was very evident to the Jews who, in amazement, charged that Jesus was: *calling God his own Father, making himself equal with God – verse 18.*

This verse also reports that: *For this reason the Jews tried all the harder to kill him.*

Could it be any clearer that the Jews saw Jesus claiming an exclusive relationship with God as His Father and that they understood this to indicate that He would be of the same nature as God? To see Jesus as the Son of God is to see Him as God.

Similarly, in **John 10:29** Jesus called God *'My Father'*. In *verse 30* He claimed *'I and the Father are one.'* This angered the Jews who picked up stones to stone Jesus. They said this was *'for blasphemy, because you a mere man, claim to be God'* – *verses 31-33.* Jesus asked, *'Why then do you accuse me of blasphemy because I said, "I am God's Son"?'* – *verse 36.*

To refer to Jesus as *'The Son of God'* is to refer to Him as *'God'*. **Hebrews 7:3** declares that the Son of God is *'without beginning of days or end of life'*. In other words, Jesus is 'the Eternal'.

John commences His gospel with a positive statement that Jesus is God; *'The Word was God.'* There are clear assertions of Christ's divinity all through the gospel and at its climax Jesus is proclaimed to be *'Lord'* and *'God'* – **John 20:28. Verse 31** states that the things highlighted in the gospel are *'written that you may believe that Jesus is the Christ, the Son of God.'*

We of the twenty-first century Western culture do not embrace the thought patterns of our spiritual forebears of two thousand years ago. We may find some of their concepts strange but we nevertheless need to become conversant with them and we need to understand them if we wish to understand Scripture. **Galatians 4:26** states that *'the Jerusalem that is above . . . is our mother.'* I don't normally think of the heavenly Jerusalem that way. If we want to be able to understand what Paul was getting at, we need to become conversant with his thought patterns. Scripture requires that we do this all the way through.

It is of more than passing interest to note, also, that the

terminology we are considering was quite prevalent in the ancient world and that it followed a similar pattern to that which we find in Scripture. Kenneth S. Wuest reports:

> *The terms THEOS 'god', and HUIOS THEOU, 'son of god', were both used in the Cult of the Caesar and were titles of the emperor.*[4]

Herbert Haag says concerning the title *'Son of God'*:

> *We find it first of all in the ancient East, especially Egypt. Here it was the Pharaoh who bore the title of 'son of (the sun) God'. He was both true God and true man. . . . As the son of God, the king was 'of one body with the father' – that is to say, the same in essence.*[5]

The apostle Paul reminds us of some very important facts which are summarized by Leon Morris:

> *Paul is so much in the habit of thinking of the Father and the Son as intimately related that he ascribes many gifts and graces indifferently to either. Thus he can speak of the gospel as the gospel of God (**Rom. 1:1**), and a few verses later as the gospel of Christ (**Rom. 1:16**). The two are so close that it doesn't matter which name is used. Nor is this an isolated instance. Forgiveness is from God (**Col. 2:13**), or from Christ (**Col. 3:13**), or from God for Christ's sake (**Eph. 4:32**). Revelation is from Jesus Christ (**Gal. 1:12**), and it is from the Father (**Gal. 1:16**). Very significant is the fact that this way of speaking is applied to the church (**Gal. 1:13; Rom. 16:16**), the Spirit (**1 Cor. 2:11; Rom. 8:9**), and the Kingdom (**Rom. 14:17; Col. 1:13**).*[6]

I find some other New Testament references intriguing

also. Please consider the following:

Colossians 1:3 *We always thank God, the Father of our Lord Jesus Christ.*

1 Peter 1:3 *Praise be to the God and Father of our Lord Jesus Christ!*

2 John 1:3 *Grace, mercy and peace from God the Father and from Jesus Christ, the Father's Son.*

Can you appreciate the exclusiveness of the Sonship of Jesus? Here we have Paul, Peter, and John, three inspired writers, all indicating their belief in the unshared Sonship of Jesus in an almost unthinking way. Not one of the three set out to teach anything. They seem just to have made introductory comments in their letters that would be quite understandable and acceptable to their readers. We who listen in learn from their remarks. We find that they accepted that Jesus had a special Sonship in His relationship with the Father.

---

[1] *The Lion Handbook to the Bible*, Lion Publishing, Herts, England, Second Revised edn.,1983, page 67.

[2] George Eldon Ladd, *A Theology of the New Testament*, Lutterworth Press, London, 1975, pages 160, 161.

[3] Lorraine Boettner, *Studies in Theology*, Presbyterian and Reformed Publishing Company, Philadelphia, 1965, pages 152, 153.

[4] Kenneth S. Wuest, *Bypaths in the Greek New Testament*, Wm. B. Eerdmans Publishing Co., Grand Rapids, Michigan, 1945, page 24.

[5] Herbert Haag, *Jesus, Son of God?* Ed. Edward Schillebeeckx and Johannes-Baptist Metz, T. & T. Clark Ltd. Edinburgh, 1982, page 31.

[6] Leon Morris, *The Lord From Heaven*, Inter-Varsity Fellowship, London, 1964, page 68.

Chapter 4

Scripture clearly states that Jesus is God

The subject of Jesus' deity has been a very contentious one down through history. Even today there are groups that deny that He is God. As we shall see, their reservations are without satisfactory foundations. We move then to a discussion of the Second Person of the Trinity that will require much more comment and the uncovering of a large body of evidence.

> *What think ye of Christ? Is the test,*
> *To try both your state and your scheme;*
> *You cannot be right in the rest,*
> *Until you think rightly of Him.*
>
> *Some take Him a creature to be,*
> *A man, or an angel at most.*
> *But they have not feelings like me,*
> *Nor know themselves wretched and lost.*
>
> *So guilty, so helpless am I,*
> *I durst not confide in His blood,*
> *Nor on His protection rely,*
> *Unless I were sure He is God.*

John Newton

There are some places in the Bible where Jesus is unquestionably referred to as God. The opening statement of John's Gospel is one of them:

John 1:1 *In the beginning was the Word, and the Word was with God, and the Word was God.*

The Word is said to have been there when all things began, He was with God, in fact He too was God. There is a definite complexity in God brought to light here. John goes on further to identify Him with God by saying in *verse 3* that *'Through him all things were made; without him nothing was made that has been made.'* There is no mistaking John's intention here. At the climax of his gospel John has Thomas proclaiming Jesus as *'my Lord and my God'* – **John 20:28.** If Jesus had not been God He surely would have rebuked Thomas but He calmly and appreciatively accepted the adulation of His disciple.

In an endeavour to escape the obvious meaning of **John 1:1** the Watchtower translation, *The New World Translation,* inserts an indefinite article before the word *'God'* at the end of the sentence. They have it *'the Word was a god'.* The first God gains a capital letter, but Jesus is just *'a god'* with a small letter. This, of course, requires us to believe in two genuine Gods. Such a belief is a miniature form of polytheism, which is paganism. The Bible knows only one true God. Reputable scholars of the Greek *New Testament* reject the rendition *'the Word was a god'* as being definitely out of harmony with Greek grammar. An example is from the pen of F. F. Bruce who was at the time of writing head of a University Department specializing in New Testament Language and Literature, and co-author William J. Martin who was then head of a university department specializing in the languages of the Old Testament:

John 1:1. Much is made by Arian amateur grammarians of the omission of the definite article with 'God' in the phrase 'And the Word was God'. Such an omission is common with nouns in a predicative construction. To have used it would have equated the Word and the Word only with God, whereas without it the force is 'And the Word was Himself God.' The article is omitted, too, on occasion in other constructions, in fact, there are four instances of it in this very chapter (verses 6, 12, 13, 18), and in John 13:3, 'God is written once without and once with the article. To translate in any one of these cases 'a god' would be totally indefensible.[1]

The Watchtower Society tried to use *A Manual Grammar of the Greek New Testament* by Dana and Mantey to support their mistranslation *'a god'*. Dr Mantey, a noted Greek scholar, was most upset by this and wrote an article *'Adulterating the Bible (Exposing a Misleading Translation).'*[2]

Murray J. Harris indicates that the word *Theos* (God): *Is applied to Jesus in seven NT passages: John 1:1, John 1:18; John 20:28, Romans 9:5, Titus 2:13, Hebrews 1:8, and 2 Peter 1:1.*[3]

> *John 1:1 In the beginning was the Word, and the Word was with God, and the Word was God.*

> *John 1:18 No-one has ever seen God, but God the One and Only, who is at the Father's side, has made him known.*

> *John 20:28 Thomas said to him, 'My Lord and my God!'*

Romans 9:5 *Theirs are the patriarchs, and from them is traced the human ancestry of Christ, who is God over all, forever praised! Amen.*

Titus 2:13, 14 *While we wait for the blessed hope – the glorious appearing of our great God and Saviour, Jesus Christ, who gave himself for us to redeem us from all wickedness and to purify for himself a people that are his very own, eager to do what is good.*

Hebrews 1:8 *But about the Son he says, 'Your throne, O God, will last for ever and ever, and righteousness will be the sceptre of your kingdom.*

2 Peter 1:1 *Simon Peter, a servant and apostle of Jesus Christ, to those who through the righteousness of our God and Saviour Jesus Christ have received a faith as precious as ours:*

The New World Translation of the Jehovah's Witnesses renders **Titus 2:13:** *We wait for the happy hope and glorious manifestation of the great God and of our Saviour Christ Jesus.*

Dr Bruce Metzger responds to this translation:

*This rendering, by separating 'the great God' from 'our Saviour Christ Jesus', overlooks a principle of Greek grammar which was detected and formulated in a rule by Granville Sharp in 1798. This rule, in brief, is that when the copulative **kai** connects two nouns of the same case, if the article precedes the first noun and is not repeated before the second noun, the latter* *always refers to the same person that is expressed or described by the first noun. This verse in Titus, there-fore, must be translated, as in fact the Revised Standard Version (1952) renders it, 'Awaiting our blessed hope, the appearing of the glory of our great God and Saviour Jesus Christ.'*[4]

John Wesley was so confident that Paul called Jesus 'God' here that he stated: *Of the great God, even our Saviour Jesus Christ – so that, if there be (according to the Arian scheme) a great God and a little God, Christ is not the little God, but the great one.*[5]

When considering this verse we need to ask ourselves, 'Who are Christians waiting for to return?' Clearly we do not wait for the appearing of the Father. We await the Second Coming of Jesus. He is the One *'who gave himself for us.' – verse 14.*

Of course Jesus is also called God in *the* Old Testament:
Isaiah 9:6 *For to us a child is born, to us a son is given, and the government will be on his shoulders. And he will be called Wonderful Counsellor, Mighty God, Everlasting Father, Prince of Peace.*

There are many other places in Scripture where He is shown to be God without actually designating Him as such. For example:
Philippians 2:6 *Who, being in very nature God, did not consider equality with God something to be grasped.*

We now need to examine some others.
JOHN 8:58 *'Before Abraham was born, I am!'*
At first glance this claim may seem only a claim to pre-

44

existence. But it is more than that. Notice the response of the Jews: *At this, they picked up stones to stone him, but Jesus hid himself, slipping away from the temple grounds.* **Verse 59.**

The Jews were very concerned to obey the law and there were only five excuses that could be used to stone Jesus:

Consulting with familiar spirits
Leviticus 20:27

Cursing (blasphemy)
Leviticus 24:10-23

False prophets who lead to idolatry
Deuteronomy 13:5-10

A stubborn son
Deuteronomy 21:18-21

Adultery and rape
Deuteronomy 22:21-24; Leviticus 20:10

It is evident that the Jews were going to stone Jesus for blasphemy. When Jesus made the astonishing claim *'I and the Father are one'* in **John 10:30, verse 31** says: *Again the Jews picked up stones to stone him.*

They clarified their objection to Jesus in **verse 33:** *'We are not stoning you for any of these,'* [miracles] *replied the Jews, 'but for blasphemy, because you, a mere man, claim to be God.'*

To those who try to make Jesus' claim to full deity in **John 8:58** a mere claim to pre-existence, it should be pointed out that if Jesus simply wished to say that He was in existence prior to Abraham, He could have said *Ego En* (I was). Instead He used the term *I Am* in the absolute sense. The expression is used with a clarifying noun in other places – example: *I am the good shepherd.* But here Jesus abruptly said *I Am* without any further clarification. There is no doubt that He was claiming to be the great *I Am* who introduced Himself to Moses. Moses met Yahweh at the burning bush and Yahweh instructed him on how to approach His people. He was to reveal Yahweh to them as the great I AM.

Exodus 3:14 *'I AM WHO I AM. This is what you are to say to the Israelites: "I AM has sent me to you."'*

It should be evident that the second *I AM* is an abbreviated form of the name given in the first instance. *I AM THAT I AM* in the Greek Septuagint translation of the Old Testament is *EGO EIMI HO ON*. Referring to **John 8:58** the great New Testament Greek scholar, Archibald Thomas Robertson, says: *Undoubtedly here Jesus claims eternal existence with the absolute phrase used of God.*[6]

Only those who wish to deny the obvious will want to try to disagree with Robertson.

If Jesus is not God, we would never expect to find the things we are coming across in Scripture. We would only expect to find the things we are discovering if Jesus *is* God. But there is more yet – much, much more.

COLOSSIANS 2:9 *For in Christ all the fulness of the deity lives in bodily form.*

The Greek word for deity here is *Theotes*. It appears in no other place in the New Testament. If Paul had wanted to refer to a divine quality residing in Jesus we would have expected him to have used the Greek word *Theiotes*. Numerous commentators could be cited to confirm that Paul is saying here that the very essence of God dwells in Christ. There is no mistaking the facts here. So once more we have clear evidence showing that Jesus is God.

[1] F. F. Bruce and William J. Martin, *Christianity Today*, 18 December 1964, page 18.

[2] Julius R. Mantey, *The Watchman Examiner*, 20 November 1952.

[3] Murray J. Harris, *Jesus as God*, Baker Book House, Grand Rapids, Michigan, 1992, page 271. This book and *Jehovah's Witnesses, Jesus Christ, and the Gospel of John*, by Robert M. Bowman, Jun, Baker Book House, Grand Rapids, Michigan, 1991, are recommended as of excellent help for the study of references to Jesus as God.

[4] Bruce Metzger, *The Jehovah's Witnesses and Jesus Christ*, page 79. This was a pamphlet reprinted from the April 1953 number of *Theology Today*.

[5] John Wesley, *Explanatory Notes Upon the New Testament*, The Epworth Press, London, 1958, page 801.

[6] Archibald Thomas Robertson, *Word Pictures in the New Testament*, Harper and Bros. Ltd., NY, 1932, Vol. V, page 158.

Chapter 5

Jesus, the pre-existent Logos

That Jesus of Nazareth lived in the land of Palestine two thousand years ago is really beyond dispute. That His life was terminated by crucifixion is supported by an enormous amount of evidence and is accepted by countless millions.

He was no ordinary man, this Jesus. In fact the apostle Paul refers to Him as much more than a man. He describes Him in a way only suited for deity:

1 Corinthians 2:8 None of the rulers of this age understood it, for if they had, they would not have crucified the Lord of glory.

No ordinary man could justifiably be afforded such an exalted title. Jesus was the Lord from heaven. It was the second member of the Trinity who came from heaven and died for us.

John commences his gospel:

John 1:1 In the beginning was the Word, and the Word was with God, and the Word was God. He was with God in the beginning.

In the Koine Greek of the New Testament *'the Word'* is

'*the Logos*'. John doesn't advise why he uses the term '*Logos*' so it is safe to assume that his readers were conversant with the word and what it stands for. Evidently, John was seeking to establish rapport with the Jews and the Gentiles by the use of this term. '*The Word*' of God brought all things into being in the beginning *(Genesis 1:3, 6, 9, 14, 20, 24)*. *Psalm 33:6* provides a summary of the work of '*the Word*': *By the word of the LORD were the heavens made.*

The paraphrases of the Old Testament (the Jewish Targums) provide further insights on the Jewish understanding of '*the Word*':

The Targumists tried to give the sense of the passage being read, and not simply to translate mechanically. These Targums were produced at a time when, from motives of reverence and from a fear of breaking the third commandment, Jews had ceased to pronounce the divine name. When they came to this name in the original the readers and translators substituted some other expression they thought more reverent, such as 'the Holy One' or 'the Name'. Sometimes they said 'the Word (Memra)'. For example, where our Bible says, 'And Moses brought forth the people out of the camp to meet God' (Exod. 19:17) the Targum reads, 'to meet the Word of God.'[1]

Obviously, the Jews would not have found the name strange. The ancient Greek philosopher Plato (around 400BC), taught that '*the Word*' served as an intermediary between the great God and His creation. About AD25 a Jewish philosopher, Philo, offered similar ideas. The comments written by George A. Turner and Julius R. Mantey on this matter are:

He (John) took a term meaningful to his readers,

both those with a Jewish background and also those with a Greek background, and gave it a new and distinctively Christian connotation. He borrowed an available container and into it placed a new content so that the world might more readily come to believe. Such is the significance of the 'Word' as used in the fourth gospel.[2]

Paul took a similar opportunity when in Athens. He introduced the Creator by referring to an altar in the city which was dedicated to *'AN UNKNOWN GOD'.* – see ***Acts 17:22ff.***

In his introduction John makes it clear that *'the Logos'* comes from the vast unsearchable ages of eternity. He was there in the beginning. The verb *'was'* is an imperfect tense indicating continued existence. In ***verse 14*** John expands his advice about *'the Word'*, telling that he became flesh and dwelt among us. So the pre-incarnate Word took on human flesh and became the unique God-Man.

He whom the world cannot enclose
In Mary's bosom doth repose;
To be a little child He deigns
Who all things by Himself sustains,
Hallelujah!

Martin Luther

Despite the fact that some, such as the Christadelphians, deny the pre-existence of Jesus, the evidence showing this to be a biblical truth is abundant. We have already seen that Jesus is God and we will later examine evidence showing that He was the Creator. As such, of course, He existed prior to His becoming man (the Incarnation). For the present a few more facts will be quite sufficient.

John 1:15 and 30 are instructive for they reveal that John the Baptist, who was six months older than Jesus, stated that Jesus existed before him. This can only mean that Jesus existed before John was born. Here are the verses concerned:

John 1:15 John testifies concerning him. He cries out, saying, 'This was he of whom I said, "He who comes after me has surpassed me because he was before me." '

John 1:30 This is the one I meant when I said, 'A man who comes after me has surpassed me because he was before me.'

That John was six months older than Jesus is evident from a perusal of Luke's gospel:

Luke 1:35, 36 The angel answered, 'The Holy Spirit will come upon you, and the power of the Most High will overshadow you. So the holy one to be born will be called the Son of God. Even Elizabeth your relative is going to have a child in her old age, and she who was said to be barren is in her sixth month.

Other revealing statements could be offered, but I find the information provided by Bible scholar Walter C. Kaiser most informative:

Now look at the phrase 'is preferred before me,' or 'ranks before me.' In Greek that word is translated in every other context in a temporal sense. I can't find one instance in all of the Greek language, not one instance in the New Testament or in any of the papyri, in which it is to be translated as a 'ranking ahead of me.' In all the cases that I'm aware of, it means 'before *me'. It occurs some thirty times in the New Testament Greek, and it is used quite extensively outside the New Testament. . . . He says that the one who comes after me **was here historically** before me, for He **existed** before me. John uses the verb 'to be' in that second instance.*[3]

Micah, when predicting the birthplace of Jesus, reported that He had been in existence from the days of eternity:

Micah 5:2 *'But you, Bethlehem Ephrathah, though you are small among the clans of Judah, out of you will come for me one who will be ruler over Israel, whose origins are from of old, from ancient times.'*

Other references which clearly reveal the pre-existence of Jesus are **Isaiah 9:6; John 8:58** (Jesus undoubtedly stated that He existed before Abraham); **17:5; Hebrews 7:1-3; 13:8; Revelation 22:13.**

There are numerous statements of Jesus where He revealed that He came down from heaven. See **John 3:13, 31; 6:38, 62; 8:23; 13:3; 16:27, 28; 17:5.**

Philippians 2:6-8 speaks of Jesus saying:

Who, being in very nature God, did not consider equality with God something to be grasped, but made himself nothing, taking the very nature of a servant, being made in human likeness. And being found in appearance as a man, he humbled himself and became obedient to death – even death on a cross.

Paul surely had the above facts in mind when he wrote to the church at Corinth:

2 Corinthians 8:9 *For you know the grace of our Lord Jesus Christ, that though he was rich, yet for our sakes he became poor.*

What a wonderful Saviour! His sacrifice was not con-
fined just to the cross. The whole process involved with the
Incarnation was a wonderful self-giving sacrifice on His
behalf. We should never cease to love and praise Him for it.

[1] Leon Morris, *The Gospel According to John*, Wm. B. Eerdmans Publishing Co.,
Grand Rapids, Michigan, 1987, page 119.
[2] George A. Turner and Julius R. Mantey, *The Gospel of John*, Wm. B. Eerdmans
Publishing Co., Grand Rapids, Michigan, (no date) page 28.
[3] Walter C. Kaiser, *The Old Testament in Contemporary Preaching*, Baker Book
House, Grand Rapids, Michigan, 1973, page 45.

Chapter 6

Jesus, the pre-existent Messenger of God

This very interesting study adds to our knowledge of Jesus and the roles He played in Old Testament times. Shakespeare once said, *'All the world's a stage and all the men and women merely players, they have their exits and their entrances, and one man in his time plays many parts.'* If this is true of men, it is certainly just as true of Jesus; in fact I would say much more so. He plays many parts in the plan of redemption, He is the Angel of the Lord later known as Michael the Archangel, He is the God-Man our Saviour, the Lamb of God, He is the one Mediator between God and man, and He is our Great High Priest.

The Angel of the Lord

Augustus H. Strong says of the Angel of the Lord: *It seems in the Old Testament, with hardly more than a single exception, to designate the pre-incarnate Logos, whose manifestations in angelic or human form foreshadowed his final coming in the flesh.*[1]

An angel is someone who functions as a messenger of

God. In Hebrew the word for angel (messenger) is *Malak*, while in Greek it is *Angelos*. Neither of the words necessarily describes the nature of those referred to. Rather, they describe their function as a messenger. Any good *Lexicon* will make this clear. The word Angel is most often used of invisible spirit creatures, but it is used in the original also of what we would term:

Messengers

Isaiah 37:9 *When he heard it, he sent messengers [Malak] to Hezekiah.*

Prophets

Haggai 1:13 *Then Haggai, the LORD'S messenger [Malak], gave this message . . . .*

Priests

Malachi 2:7 *'For the lips of a priest ought to preserve knowledge, and from his mouth men should seek instruction – because he is the messenger [Malak] of the LORD Almighty.'*

John the Baptist is described as an angel in the prophecy of **Malachi 3:1; cp. Matthew 11:10:**

Malachi 3:1 *'See I will send my messenger [Malak], who will prepare the way before me.'*

Matthew 11:10 *'This is the one about whom it is written: "I will send my messenger [Angelos] ahead of you, who will prepare your way before you."'*

The scouts sent by Joshua into the Promised Land are referred to as angels in **James 2:25.** So are the men sent to

Jesus by John in *Luke 7:24;* and those whom Jesus sent ahead of Him on one occasion – *Luke 9:52.*

Genesis 16:7-14 tells of an encounter Hagar had with the Angel of the Lord. The Angel of the Lord speaks to her but in *verse 13* we are told that it was Yahweh (LORD) who spoke to her.

In *Exodus 3:1-5* the Angel of the Lord is again identified as Yahweh.

Exodus 13:21 informs us that it was Yahweh who went before Israel at the time of the Exodus from Egypt, while *Exodus 14:19, 20* advises that it was the Angel of the Lord who did so. *Verse 24* reminds us again that it is Yahweh of whom we are reading. See also *Isaiah 63:9.*

When we come to the New Testament we discover that it was Jesus who accompanied the Israelites:

> *1 Corinthians 10:3, 4 They all ate the same spiritual food and drank the same spiritual drink; for they drank from the spiritual rock that accompanied them, and that rock was Christ.*

An examination of *Judges 2:1-5* also reveals the Angel of the Lord to be Yahweh.

Joshua 5:13-6:2 concerns an Angel who describes himself as *'commander of the army of the LORD* [Yahweh]' and He speaks to Joshua. *Chapter 6:2* reveals that in reality it was Yahweh who was speaking. Notice also that *chapter 5:15* contains a command similar to that given to Moses at the burning bush *(Exodus 3:5)*. This also assures us that the Angel was God Himself:

> *Joshua 5:15 The commander of the LORD'S army replied, 'Take off your sandals, for the place where you are standing is holy.' And Joshua did so.*

The Archangel Michael

M. Bouttier contributed the article 'Angel' to J. J. Von Allmen's *Vocabulary of the Bible*. He states on page 18 that after the Jewish exile: *The ancient 'angel of the Lord', henceforth will bear the name of Michael (**Dan. 12:1**)*.

While in extra-biblical literature seven Archangels are named, the Bible knows of only one Archangel, His name is Michael. The name 'Michael' means 'who is like God?'[2]

The name has been taken as a suggestion of the deity of Michael. This is quite an acceptable suggestion in the light of all the other evidence. If we explore further the title 'Commander of the army of the LORD', we find that in other contexts His name is sometimes Michael and sometimes it is Jesus.

Revelation 12:7-9 reveal that the leader of God's angels is Michael. Here we read of *'Michael and his angels'*. When we compare *Matthew 16:27* we find that the heavenly angels belong to Jesus – they are *His* angels. The obvious conclusion is that Jesus is Michael. ***Revelation 19:11-16*** confirms that Jesus leads the angelic forces – *'the armies of heaven were following him'* – ***verse 14.***

No special mental powers are necessary for us to see that the *'commander of the army of the Lord'*, Michael the Archangel (chief of the Angels), and Jesus (*'his angels'*), are the same Person. This conclusion may sound strange to ears formerly unaware of the fact, but prominent Christians such as Martin Luther, John Calvin, Matthew Henry, Hengstenberg, Fairbairn, and numerous others have also identified Michael as Jesus.

Michael the Archangel is referred to by name only three times in the Old Testament and twice in the New Testament. The term *'the archangel Michael'* is used with reference to him only at ***Jude 9.*** In ***Revelation 12*** he is just called

Michael. He is referred to merely as *'the archangel'* in *1 Thessalonians 4:16.*

The following is a brief appraisal of the six passages concerned:

Daniel 10:13 'But the prince of the Persian kingdom resisted me twenty-one days. Then Michael, one of the chief princes, came to help me, because I was detained there with the king of Persia.'

Here Michael is referred to as a *'prince'*. This does not limit him to the nature, or level, of other princes mentioned in the chapter. In *Daniel 12:1* Michael is referred to as *'the great prince who protects your people'*. Jesus is the one who protects the people of God and the term *'prince'* is a common designation for Him in the book of *Daniel* – see *chapter 8:11, 25* and *9:25* (King James Version). It was not inappropriate in *Daniel 10,* where the unseen spirit leaders of the nations are described as *'princes',* for Jesus (Michael), who stands for the people of God, to be likewise included as one of them.

Daniel 10:21 'No one supports me against them except Michael, your prince.' Here Michael is specifically designated Israel's prince.

Daniel 12:1 'At that time Michael, the great prince who protects your people, will arise.'

Michael is clearly seen here as the protector of God's people. Surely this must be Jesus being referred to, for the whole tenor of Scripture points to Him as being our Protector, our Deliverer, our King, our Saviour. *Daniel 12:1*, which portrays Michael as the chief actor in the final time of trouble, should be compared with *Revelation 19:11-21* where Jesus is revealed as the chief agent of God at that time.

Jude 9 But even the archangel Michael, when he was

disputing with the devil about the body of Moses, did not dare to bring a slanderous accusation against him, but said, 'The Lord rebuke you!'

This verse is not suggesting that Jesus (Michael) was too afraid to rebuke Satan, but rather that it was out of character for Him to do so, that is, in the slanderously accusing way of those referred to in **verses 8** and **10**. Jesus simply said to Satan what He said as the Angel of the Lord in **Zechariah 3:2**. The following are **verses 1** and **2** of that chapter:

Then he showed me Joshua the high priest standing before the angel of the LORD, and Satan standing at his right side to accuse him. The LORD said to Satan, 'The LORD rebuke you, Satan!'

Revelation 12:7 *And there was war in heaven. Michael and his angels fought against the dragon, and the dragon and his angels fought back.*

The leader of God's forces in heaven is seen here in conflict with the devil and his forces. Surely no one less than Jesus is meant!

1 Thessalonians 4:16 *For the Lord himself will come down from heaven, with a loud command, with the voice of the archangel and with the trumpet call of God, and the dead in Christ will rise first.*

It is quite legitimate to accept that *'the voice of the archangel'* which summons the righteous dead to arise from their graves is the voice of the descending Jesus. W. E. Vine says: *In 1 Thess. 4:16 the meaning seems to be that the voice of the Lord Jesus will be of the character of an archangelic shout.*[3]

John 5:28, 29 *'Do not be amazed at this, for a time is coming when all who are in their graves will hear his voice* *and come out – those who have done good will rise to live, and those who have done evil will rise to be condemned.'*

These verses clearly advise that it is at the voice of Jesus that the dead are raised. His voice and the Archangel's voice must be the same.

Already we are noticing that God is not a solitary Being but rather there is a complexity to His make-up; but we must wait for further clarification in the latter section of this book.

----

[1] Augustus H. Strong, *Systematic Theology*, The Judson Press, Valley Forge, PA. 1907, page 95.

[2] *Baker's Encyclopedia of the Bible*, Baker Book House, Grand Rapids, Michigan, 1988, Vol. 2, page 1454.

[3] W. E. Vine, *An Expository Dictionary of New Testament Words*, Oliphants Ltd., London, 1946, Vol. 1, page 72.

Chapter 7

Jesus, the Creator

Under this heading we will show that Jesus is the Creator. I have seen the smiles of pleasant surprise on the faces of many when I have helped them to understand, for the first time, that Jesus is the Creator.

John 1:3 says: *Through him all things were made; without him nothing was made that has been made.*

Hebrews 1:2 reports that the universe was made through Jesus.

Colossians 1:16, 17 reveal that: By *him all things were created: things in heaven and on earth, visible and invisible, whether thrones or powers or rulers or authorities; all things were created by him and for him. He is before all things, and in him all things hold together.*

What more needs to be said? He created all things, therefore He cannot be a created 'thing' Himself. Not only did He create all things but also they were created 'for him'. Not for someone else, mind you, but for Himself. And that's not all – He also sustains 'all things'. In other words, He keeps everything going. He alone who created is able to sustain. As the songwriter aptly put it, *'He's got the whole world in His hands'*. We are entirely dependent upon Him.

Every heartbeat is a signal that He is there and that He cares for us. The One we are speaking of is Jesus our Saviour. Can you really explain why this One, the great King of the Universe, should come and be crucified by His creatures; dying the most vile kind of death for us? The answer is because of His indescribable, unfathomable love. Could He have shown His love for us in a more appealing way? How comforting to know that:

> *'The helm of the universe is held by the hands which were pierced for us'* – *Alexander MacLaren.*

Some, like the Jehovah's Witnesses, claim that Jesus was like a Foreman on a construction site. He only created on behalf of Jehovah and that He is not Jehovah. Amazing, is it not, that some will go directly against clear statements of Scripture? Doesn't **Colossians 1:16** say *'all things were created by him and for him'?* See chapter 9 for more on **Colossians 1:15ff**.

According to Robert Morey, **Ecclesiastes 12:1** literally refers to *'Creators'.*[1]

This plural is tremendously interesting! It is what Scripture clearly teaches. Please consider carefully the following:

> **Isaiah 44:24** *'This is what the LORD says – your Redeemer, who formed you in the womb: I am the LORD, who has made all things, who alone stretched out the heavens, who spread out the earth by myself.'*

In summary, this is what this verse reports:
- Yahweh states that **He made all things.**
- He **alone stretched out the heavens.**
- Additionally, **He spread out the earth by Himself.**

How important it is then to note what God says to Jesus

(the Son) concerning His involvement in creation:

Hebrews 1:10 '*In the beginning, O Lord, you laid the foundations of the earth, and the heavens are the work of your hands.*'

Of course the divine name Yahweh (not 'Jehovah' which the Witnesses say must be proclaimed all over the world) is rendered here as LORD. Yahweh is saying that He made all things. On His own He stretched out the heavens and by Himself He spread out the earth. How can anyone honestly claim that Yahweh had a Foreman (or someone similar) as a helper? There is no contradiction for those who know the truth about the Trinity. Jesus is a member of the Godhead and as such was the Creator. Yahweh was the Old Testament name for the Triune God.

We will observe the undeniable fact that Jesus was involved in Creation. Chapter ten, the section, 'The Holy Spirit was involved with Creating', will show that He also took a part. When all the evidence is taken into account there is no escaping the conclusion that the Father, the Son, and the Holy Spirit were all involved in Creation and are therefore the Yahweh of the Old Testament. Another unquestionable proof of the Trinity is locked up in these facts.

---

[1] Robert Morey, *THE TRINITY Evidences and Issues*, World Publishing, Grand Rapids, Michigan, page 93.

Chapter 8

Other indicators of the deity of Jesus

The list could go on and on. We will nevertheless review quite a few more indicators of Jesus' deity. However, I will make my comments as brief as possible.

Jesus shares the glory of Yahweh

Isaiah 42:8 *'I am the LORD; that is my name! I will not give my glory to another.' (See also **Isaiah 48:11**.)*

John 17:5 *'And now, Father, glorify me in your presence with the glory I had with you before the world began.'*

Yahweh stated emphatically that He would not give His glory to another. We find, however, that Jesus does share this glory and this confirms that He shares a place in the Trinity – Yahweh.

Jesus is King of kings, and Lord of lords

Paul applies these titles to God in *1 Timothy 6:15* and John credits Jesus with them in *Revelation 17:14* and *19:16*. While pagan kings may have claimed these titles, there is only one 'King of kings and Lord of lords' really.

The conclusion, then, is obvious.

Statements revealing the deity of Jesus in the book of Revelation

Speaking of God, *1 Kings 8:39* states: *'You alone know the hearts of all men.'*

Compare with this *Psalm 7:9* and *Romans 8:27.* We cannot deny that Jesus is God when in one of the letters He was dictating to the seven churches of Revelation He clearly says: *'All the churches will know that I am he who searches hearts and minds'* – *Revelation 2:23.*

Revelation 14:4 says that the 144,000 are *'offered as firstfruits to God and the Lamb'.* The *'firstfruits'* were an offering to God – see *Exodus 23:19.* Such an offering would not be made to the Lamb unless He was God also.

Revelation 20:6 states that those brought to life in the first resurrection will be *'priests of God and of Christ'.* How could they be associated as priests of God and of Christ if Christ is not God?

Revelation 22:13 will be the final text I will refer to under this heading, although there are certainly others. At *Isaiah 44:6* Yahweh says: *'I am the first and I am the last'* – see also *48:12.*

What can we say when we find Jesus reporting, in *Revelation 22:13, 'I am the Alpha and the Omega, the First and the Last, the Beginning and the End'?* Can we say less than that He must be God?

A comparison of Old Testament and New Testament passages which clearly reveal the deity of Jesus

I offer the following verses for comparison, for they show without doubt that Jesus is the Yahweh of the Old Testament. Of course the Father is also Yahweh and, as we will see later, the Spirit is also Yahweh. There are not three Yahwehs though – just One.

A comparison of many Old Testament passages with New Testament passages makes it crystal clear that the New Testament writers applied them to Jesus Christ. This is magnificent testimony to the deity of Jesus. The following are examples, but please check them for yourself in order to gain their full import:

Psalm 102:24-27; Hebrews 1:8-12
'In the beginning you laid the foundations of the earth, and the heavens are the work of your hands.'

Isaiah 6:3
'Holy, holy, holy is the LORD Almighty; the whole earth is full of his glory.'

John 12:36-41
Isaiah said this because he saw Jesus' glory and spoke about him.

Psalm 34:8; 1 Peter 2:3
Taste and see that the LORD is good.

1 Kings 8:39; Revelation 2:23
You alone know the hearts of all men.

Isaiah 44:6; Revelation 22:13
'I am the first and I am the last'

Joel 2:32; Romans 10:13
'Everyone who calls on the name of the LORD will be saved.'

Please note that if you view **Romans 10:13** in the *New World Translation* of the Jehovah's Witnesses you will find that it imposes the name Jehovah there in order to disguise the obvious meaning that we will be saved if we call upon the name of Jesus.

Compare **Psalm 68:18** with **Ephesians 4:8, 9**

Compare **Isaiah 8:12, 13** with **1 Peter 3:14, 15**

Astonishing things Jesus said and did

The best advice that could be given would be to request a reading of the four gospels. Among the many amazing things to be noted there are the following few selections:

In **Matthew 10:37-39** Jesus insisted that we must love Him above all others. In fact, we are expected to follow Him even to the point of losing our lives if this is necessary – and this for His sake. Surely this is a claim on us that no one less than God should make? Why should we love Jesus to this extent if He is not God? If He was not God, should He not have directed our love to God?

Jeremiah 17:5 and **Psalm 146:3** warn against trusting in men and yet Jesus invites us, *'Come unto me, all you who are weary and burdened, and I will give you rest'* – *Matthew 11:28.* If He had said this in the hearing of those not His followers, surely they would have accused Him of blasphemy? Such claims upon men came naturally to Jesus. Without hesitation He often placed Himself on an equality with God:

'If anyone loves me, he will obey my teaching. My Father will love him, and we will come to him and make our home with him' – **John 14:23.**

How incongruous would it seem if someone else, let us say Abraham, Moses, Peter, Paul, James, or John, had spoken in this manner? But they were only men and Jesus was not, and so we feel no surprise.

The prophets all spoke with a *'thus sayeth the Lord'*. Jesus says, *'But I tell you'* – **Matthew 5:28, 32, 34, 39,** and **44.** At the end of the Sermon on the Mount He referred to the instructions He had given as *'these words of mine'* – **Matthew 7:24, 26.** Not long before His crucifixion He said, *'Heaven and earth will pass away, but my words will never pass away'* – **Matthew 24:35.** What an astounding claim! But praise God His words are true.

One thing that really astonished the Jews and aroused their anger was the act of forgiving sins by Jesus. **Isaiah 43:25** shows this to be the prerogative of God: *'I, even I, am he who blots out your transgressions, for my own sake, and remembers your sins no more.'*

The Jews, of course, knew this to be true. Luke reports an instance of Jesus' forgiving sins and the response of some of the Jews:

Luke 5:20, 21 *When Jesus saw their faith, he said, 'Friend, your sins are forgiven.' The Pharisees and the teachers of the law began thinking to themselves, 'Who is this fellow who speaks blasphemy? Who can forgive sins but God alone?'*

It is patently clear that Jesus had no right to act and speak as He did on many occasions unless He was God. His followers recognized who He was; they even attributed the power they had to heal to Him – **Acts 3:6.**

Jesus demonstrated His power over nature by walking on the water – **Matthew 14:26-33.** He also calmed the wind and sea – **Mark 4:39-41.**

Jesus is Omnipresent, Omniscient, and Omnipotent

Jesus claimed *Omnipresence* by stating that: *'Where two or three come together in my name, there am I with them'* – *Matthew 18:20.* See also *28:20* and *John 14:23.*

Jesus is *Omniscient* (all knowing). Peter acknowledged this under inspiration: *'Lord you know all things.'* – *John 21:17.*

He used His omniscience on several occasions and these examples provide thrilling reading:

Jesus told Nathaniel, *'I saw you while you were still under the fig-tree before Philip called you'* – *John 1:48.* The woman at the well was amazed that this man knew all about her and said, *'Come, see a man who told me everything I ever did'* – *John 4:29.* Jesus told the royal official at Cana that his son would live. The son did live and the father discovered that he had recovered at the exact time Jesus said that he would – *John 4:46-53.* Jesus knew that His friend Lazarus had died while He was days away from where he lived – *John 11:11-14.* He was able to instruct His disciples to *'Go to the village ahead of you, and just as you enter it, you will find a colt tied there, which no-one has ever ridden'* – *Mark 11:2.* Please also read *Mark 14:13-16* and *Matthew 17:27.*

The *Omnipotence* of Jesus has already been demonstrated – He is the Creator, and the preservation of all things requires omnipotence *(John 1:3; Colossians 1:16, 17; Hebrews 1:3).*

Jesus accepts worship

Only God deserves our worship and He only is entitled to it. The devil tries to induce creatures to worship him. He even tried to entice Jesus to offer him worship but Jesus rebuked him, saying:

Matthew 4:10 *'Away from me, Satan! For it is written: "Worship the Lord your God, and serve him only."'*

Angels of God refuse to accept worship, as can be seen in the record of **Revelation 19:10** and **22:8, 9.**

After Jesus walked on the water the disciples worshipped Him. Here is what the record says: *Then those who were in the boat worshipped him, saying, 'Truly you are the Son of God.'* – **Matthew 14:33.**

The final verses of the gospel of Luke refer to the last moments Jesus spent on earth: *When he had led them out to the vicinity of Bethany, he lifted up his hands and blessed them. While he was blessing them, he left them and was taken up into heaven. Then they worshipped him and returned to Jerusalem with great joy.* – **Luke 24:50-52.**

There are other instances where the followers of Jesus worshipped Him. Shortly after His resurrection Jesus met some of them: *They came to him, clasped his feet and worshipped him.* – **Matthew 28:9.**

While Jesus reprimanded Satan for craving worship, Jesus Himself readily accepted it. This must surely be accepted by us as an acknowledgment, on His part, of His deity.

Exodus 34:14 *Do not worship any other god.*

Hebrews 1:6 *And again, when God brings his firstborn into the world, he says, 'Let all God's angels worship him.'*

Several indications of the worship of Jesus are found in the Book of Revelation. Millard J. Erickson provides a perceptive comment on this:

The Book of Revelation, which gives us more glimpses of worship than any other New Testament book, shows us several examples of worship of the Lord, in an eschatological setting. In 5:8-14 there is a progression of worshippers of the Lamb, expanding outward. First the four living creatures and the twenty-four elders fall down before the Lamb (v. 8) in the traditional posture of worship. Then they sing a hymn of praise to the Lamb (vv. 9-10). It is apparent from what they sing, regarding his worthiness to receive praise because he was slain and by his blood has purchased men for God from every tribe and language and people and nation, that this lamb is Jesus Christ. Next, in verse 12 a huge number of angels also sing to this lamb. Then every creature 'in heaven and on earth and under the earth and on the sea, and all that is in them' join in the song (v. 13); the four living creatures say 'Amen' and the elders fall down and worship.[1]

A brief summary. Scripture reveals that men, even angels, worship Jesus. Jesus accepts this. However, He rebuked Satan for desiring it. Worship is strictly forbidden of all but God. The angels are directed to worship Jesus. Surely if angels worship Jesus, it goes without saying that man, as a lesser creature, should do likewise. Isn't it painfully obvious that Jesus is God?

Jesus accepts prayer

In *Acts 7:59* we find Stephen at the point of being stoned to death: *While they were stoning him, Stephen prayed, 'Lord Jesus, receive my spirit.' Then he fell on his knees and cried out, 'Lord, do not hold this sin against them.'*

Next we peruse *2 Corinthians 12:8, 9: Three times I pleaded with the Lord to take it away from me. But he said to me, 'My grace is sufficient for you, for my power is made perfect in weakness.' Therefore I will boast all the more gladly about my weaknesses, so that Christ's power may rest on me.*

We cannot but conclude that Paul testified that he prayed

to Jesus three times about his 'thorn in the flesh'.

In *John 14:14* Jesus encouraged us to pray to Him, saying: *'You may ask me for anything in my name, and I will do it.'*

Who could deny that at the very end of the book of Revelation we have a prayer of John to Jesus: *Come, Lord Jesus – 22:20.*

Calling upon the name of Jesus

In connection with the study of worship and prayer to Jesus, it is profitable to study the phrase 'call upon the name'. An examination of Old Testament passages reveals that it is linked with the act of worship:

Genesis 12:8 Abraham *built an altar to the LORD and called on the name of the LORD.*

Psalm 116:17 *I will sacrifice a thank-offering to you and call on the name of the LORD.*

Joel 2:32 points to a future day when *everyone who calls on the name of the LORD will be saved.*

This latter passage is applied by the apostle Paul to Jesus: *'Everyone who calls on the name of the Lord will be saved.' – Romans 10:13.*

Here is further indisputable evidence that Jesus is Yahweh. Complete confidence in, and devotion to, Jesus is necessary for salvation.

In an obvious endeavour to divert attention from the fact that Jesus is Yahweh, the Watchtower's *The New World Translation* inserts the name Jehovah in **Romans 10:13** in lieu of the name Lord. The context leaves no doubt that it is Jesus who is being referred to. Fortunately, there are several other places in the New Testament where this descriptive phrase is carried over from the Old Testament and applied to Jesus. No clearer statement on the matter could be desired than that found in *1 Corinthians 1:2:* . . . *together with all those everywhere who call on the name of our Lord Jesus Christ – their Lord and ours.*

Christians were well known as those who called upon the name of Jesus. This can easily be seen from the experience of Paul. After his conversion Paul *began to preach in the synagogues that Jesus is the Son of God. All those who heard him were astonished and asked, 'Isn't he the man who caused havoc in Jerusalem among those who call on this name?' Acts 9:20, 21.* See also *verses 13, 14.*

Conclusion on the deity of Jesus

After I refused to be any longer influenced by the Watchtower Society, I really began to understand the Scriptures. As I studied I found myself overwhelmed by the evidence for the deity of Jesus. How could I honestly deny all of the above? I have to say that if Jesus was not God He deserved an Oscar! If He was not what He claimed to be He was either mad, or bad. The conclusion is inescapable, Jesus was a liar, a lunatic, or He was Lord (God). C. S. Lewis put it this way:

A man who was merely a man and said the sort of things Jesus said would not be a great moral teacher. He would either be a lunatic – on a level with the man who says he is a poached egg – or else he would be the Devil of Hell. You must make your choice. Either this man was, and is, the Son of God: or else a madman or something worse. You can shut Him up for a fool, you can spit at him and kill Him as a demon; or you can fall at His feet and call Him Lord and God. But let us not come with any patronising nonsense about His being a great human teacher. He has not left that open to us. He did not intend to.[2]

---

[1] Millard J. Erickson, *God in Three Persons*, Baker Books, Grand Rapids, Michigan, 1995, page 315.
[2] C. S. Lewis, *Mere Christianity*, Collins, Fontana Books, London, 1964, pages 52, 53.

Chapter 9

Answers to objections to the deity of Jesus

O
ur study so far has shown that the Scriptures refer to Jesus in the most exalted way possible. He is God – He is Yahweh – He is the Creator – He sustains all things – He is to be worshipped. Nevertheless, there are some passages of Scripture which refer to Him as though He were less than God. It is true that the Bible does contain some paradoxical statements in its references to Jesus.

Never let us forget that Jesus was a Person with a dual nature! He was the God-Man. Remember that the Word, who was God, became flesh and dwelt among us (*John 1:1, 14*). Of course God cannot cease being God. It is not surprising, then, that some passages refer to His deity while others relate to His humanity. The Divine Word never ceased to be – He became incarnate as Jesus of Nazareth. He was at the same time the Son of God and the Son of Man. In the words of Robert Clarke:

> *Christ on earth was just as much God as though not at all man, and just as much man as though He were not at all God.*

What Clarke says is unquestionably true – but to try to understand the complexity of the God-Man is beyond the capacity of the human mind. Further to that, we simply don't have the information necessary even if we *did* have the ability to comprehend this unique situation. When we keep these facts in mind we can understand that when He was a man Jesus had a God and He prayed to Him. In His role as the Mediator during the plan of Salvation Jesus accepted a lower position than the Father and this explains some situations that provide difficulty for some objectors. It is hard to see how anyone can deny that one member of the Trinity could accept a subordinate position if He was agreeable. As we view some verses which may seem to be difficult, we need to ask ourselves, 'Does this verse apply to the **nature** of Christ? Or, does it apply to His **position?**' If this rule is applied, a lot of seemingly difficult passages will be seen to provide little cause for concern.

We need to be quite clear on this. Let us suppose that our Prime Minister is to go on a mission to another country. He may say he has been sent by the people of Great Britain for such and such a reason. First of all let us ask, is the Prime Minister any different from us by nature because of his position? Of course not. Is he any less than we are by nature because we have sent him? No, again. When Jesus accepted our nature He assumed a lesser position than the Father but He was no less than God by nature.

Because the Bible requires us to believe that God is a Trinity we can accept that, for the purposes of the plan of redemption, the Father, the Son, and the Holy Spirit decided, in the Councils of the Godhead, to accept various positions in conducting the plan. The Father accepted what we might call the position of 'Managing-Architect', Jesus accepted the position of 'Mediator-Redeemer', and the

Holy Spirit accepted the position of 'Comforter-Sanctifier'. Jesus was sent on the mission of redemption by the Father, subsequently the Holy Spirit was sent by both the Father and the Son (Jesus) to draw attention to what Jesus had done for us and to work to restore men to the image of God. In this light there can be said to be priority of position in the Godhead. The Father is spoken of as the First Person, the Son the Second Person, and the Holy Spirit the Third Person. These positions do not imply any superiority or inferiority of Nature and could be assumed without any difficulty because the Members of the Trinity are in perfect unity.

In the light of the above, let us consider some texts that are sometimes offered as objections to Jesus' being God.

- **Objection** – *John 12:44.* Here Jesus is said to have been *sent* by God.

  Answer: A problem? Not in the light of the above!

- **Objection** – *John 14:28.* Jesus said, *'the Father is greater than I.'*

  Answer: If Jesus was just a man He would have sounded absolutely foolish for stating the obvious. There is no doubt that Jesus was referring to His position (not nature) here. When He returned to the Father He would then be in a better position to help them. The Holy Spirit would be sent to them then. While He remained a man there was a limit to what He could do.

- **Objection** – *Mark 10:18:* *'Why do you call me good?'* *Jesus answered. 'No-one is good – except God alone.'* Jesus was obviously denying that He was God.

  Answer: There are several possible answers to this alleged problem.

Jesus could have meant, *'There is really only one who is good and that is God. By calling me good, are you acknowledging that I am God?'*

On the other hand Jesus may have been concerned that the man was using the word 'good' lightly. The only one who is really good is God. He did not want to be called God ('good') unless the man really understood Him to be such. Jesus did not go about just making claims, He wanted people to believe in Him because of the evidence, not because of any claim He might have made. Likewise, He did not want anyone to accept that He was God unless it was on the basis of the evidence available to them.

Then again, Jesus may have meant, *Don't go around using the word **good** loosely. Compare what you consider to be good with God. He is the ultimate in goodness. This being the case the word should not be used indiscriminately.*

Jesus was not saying that He was not God.

- **Objection** – *John 17:3 'This is eternal life: that they may know you, the only true God, and Jesus Christ, whom you have sent.'* Jesus' statement shows that He is not God.

Answer: If Jesus was talking of His relationship with the Father there might be some substance to the objection here. The suggestion is that Jesus here excludes Himself from being part of the *'only true God'*. What we have before us here is part of Jesus' High Priestly prayer. His relationship with the Father is not in view. We have Jesus on earth praying to the Father in heaven and He is emphasizing the need for people to recognize the only true God as opposed to idols and other false gods. Also, the need for recognition of Himself as the means of salvation. We must always take the context into account, and what the Bible says in other places. For example *1 John 5:20* calls Jesus *'the true God and eternal life'*.

The comments on *1 Corinthians 8:6* below are also significant here.

- **Objection** – *1 Corinthians 11:3* states that *the head of every man is Christ, and the head of the woman is man, and the head of Christ is God.* The objector claims that Christ cannot be God because God is His head.

  Answer: This is a classic example of someone not taking into account the fact that *position* is in question here – not *nature*. While man is the head of the woman they are not different by nature. Christ, in his role as Mediator-Redeemer, comes under the headship of God.

- **Objection** - *1 Timothy 2:5* states, *For there is one God and one mediator between God and men, the man Christ Jesus.* Therefore, some say, Jesus is not God but the mediator.

  Answer: Quite to the contrary – it has been well said that a mediator must be the equal of either of the two parties between whom he mediates. It has also been claimed, and I agree with the claim, *'Being God, Jesus can perfectly represent God to men, and being man He can perfectly represent man to God.'* Only by being God can Jesus fully comprehend the claims of God and only by being man can Jesus fully comprehend the needs of men. Because He is God Jesus can reveal God to us. Please note the following verses:

  John 1:18 *No-one has ever seen God, but God the One and Only, who is at the Father's side, has made him known.*

  John 14:9 *'Anyone who has seen me has seen the Father.'*

We see Jesus, in His role as Mediator, making the Book of Revelation available to us:

Revelation 1:1 The revelation of Jesus Christ, which God gave him to show his servants what must soon take place.

- **Objection** – *1 Corinthians 8:6* says, *For us there is but one God, the Father, from whom all things came and for whom we live; and there is but one Lord Jesus Christ, through whom all things came and through whom we live.*

Answer: If this verse precludes Jesus from being God, because it says only the Father is God, it must also preclude the Father from being Lord because it says that Jesus is the only Lord! If we remember *John 20:28* we find there that Jesus is called both *Lord* and *God*.

If we study *1 Corinthians 8:6* we find that Paul is talking about idols and food sacrificed to them. A closer look will reveal that *verses 5* and *6* are parenthetical and are an elaboration of *verse 4* which says, *'There is no God but one.'* In this parenthesis Paul elaborates on the statement just made and says in *verse 6, 'There is no God but one . . . and there is but one Lord, Jesus Christ.'* If Paul did not think of Jesus as being God, why did he mention Him in this context? Was he trying to prove that only one God exists by demonstrating that he had two?

There is plenty of evidence available to show that Paul's mention of the Father and Jesus together is typical of his thinking of their oneness or unity. He always thought of God the Father and the Lord Jesus Christ together. Please read closely the following from the excellent chapter 'God Our Father and the Lord Jesus Christ', written by B. B. Warfield:

In the opening sentence of the very first of Paul's let-
ters which have come down to us – and that is as much
as to say, in the very first sentence which, so far as we
know, he ever wrote, – he makes use of a phrase in
speaking of the Christian's God, which at once
attracts our interested attention.

According to the generous way he had of thinking
and speaking of his readers at the height of their pro-
fessions, he describes the church at Thessalonica as
living and moving and having its being in God. But, as
it was a Christian church which he was addressing, he
does not content himself, in this description, with the
simple term 'God'. He uses the compound phrase
'God the Father and the Lord Jesus Christ'. The
Thessalonians, he says, because they were Christians,
lived and moved and had their being 'in God the
Father and the Lord Jesus Christ'.

It is quite clear that this compound phrase was not
new on Paul's lips, coined for this occasion. It bears
on its face the evidence of a long and familiar use, by
which it had been worn down to its bare bones. All the
articles have been rubbed off, and with them all other
accessories; and it stands out in its baldest elements
as just 'God Father and Lord Jesus Christ.' Plainly we
have here a mode of speaking of the Christians' God
which was customary with Paul.[1]

Warfield also says:
That we may see at a glance how clear it is that Paul
is making use here of a fixed formula in his desig-
nation of the Christians' God, and may observe at the
same time the amount of freedom which he allows him-
self in repeating it in these very formal prayers, we

bring together the series of these opening prayers, in the chronological order of the epistles in which they occur.[2]

He then quotes *1 Thessalonians 1:1; 2 Thessalonians 1:2; Galatians 1:3; 1 Corinthians 1:3; 2 Corinthians 1:2; Romans 1:7; Ephesians 1:2; 6:23; Colossians 1:2; Philemon 3; Philippians 1:2; 1 Timothy 1:2; Titus 1:4; 2 Timothy 1:2.* This formula was also utilized by others – *James 1:1; 2 Peter 1:2; 2 John 3.* For the point being made to make its true impact all of these verses need to be viewed. Please read them.

Those who have followed the above evidence closely will surely agree that when Paul said, *'there is no God but one,'* he immediately thought of this God in the way He always thought of Him, i.e. *'God the Father and the Lord Jesus Christ.'*

The discerning comments of I. Howard Marshall are important for consideration here:

The New Testament does not often call Jesus God directly, but it certainly takes over the Old Testament use of Kupios to refer to God and reapplies it to Jesus. Passages of Scripture that originally applied to God are reapplied to Jesus, thereby showing a tacit identi-fication of Jesus with the Lord spoken of in the Old Testament. So much so is this the case that it is true to say that the word 'Lord' in a religious sense is applied to Jesus more often than to God the Father in the New Testament. It appears that the Christians needed a new terminology to express the place of Jesus alongside God. They had two solutions. One was to speak of Jesus as the Son alongside the Father; the other was to appropriate one of the titles for God, namely Lord, for him and to reserve the title of God for the Father, and by and large they kept to this use of the titles. [3]

Objections such as this may at first appear to be sound but in the light of a study of the context and the usage of the phrase in question by Paul it is of no value to the objector.

- **Objection** – *Mark 13:32 'No one knows about that day or hour, not even the angels in heaven, nor the Son, but only the Father.'* In the light of this verse Jesus cannot be said to be God.

Answer: The objector emphasizes that Jesus doesn't know the time of the Second Coming but the Father does – therefore, it is claimed, Jesus cannot be God.

It is wise to say that this is a problem for which no answer is given and therefore we will not say more than that in his humanity Jesus did not have information on this matter. Jesus was a man and it simply is not given to men to know such things. Please compare *Acts 1:6, 7* on this. This is ultimately the conclusion we must come to; however, for the sake of showing the reasonableness of this, we will explore the matter further.

There is no doubt that when the Word became flesh *(John 1:14)*, His deity was veiled; His humanity was real. Speaking of Him as a child, *Luke 2:52* says: *And Jesus grew in wisdom and stature, and in favour with God and men.*

The fact that He was very human is emphasized by texts that tell us that He knew weariness *(John 4:6);* was hungry *(Matthew 21:18)* and thirsty *(John 19:28)*. Yet on other occasions the Scriptures inform us that He possessed remarkable knowledge and ability. Please read again the texts I cited under the heading 'Jesus is Omnipresent,

Omniscient, and Omnipotent', regarding His Omniscience, found on page 69.

It is obvious that while a man, Jesus was very dependent upon the Father because His deity was veiled. On occasions He possessed incredible knowledge unavailable to normal men. Paradoxically, He was also ignorant of things which were known to God. How can all this be reconciled? We need to recognize that Jesus, as a man, had a finite mode of consciousness. However, because He was God, He had at the same time an infinite mode of consciousness. This being the case, we have the problem of trying to understand how these two opposites, infinite knowledge and finite knowledge, could co-exist in the God-Man. I appreciate the helpful advice of Alan N. Stibbs on this matter:

When we try . . . to appreciate how two such apparently contradictory conditions may actively co-exist in a single personality it is possible, for what it is worth, as Charles Harris indicates, to obtain some suggestive help to our thinking from inferior analogies. For instance, while his conscious mind is otherwise engaged, a person's subconscious mind (without his conscious knowledge) may think out a problem of which it has previously been made aware; so that, when he returns later to his mental task, the solution of the problem instantly appears. Similarly, after being hypnotized, a person who returns to normal control may be said to be 'ignorant' of things experienced or learnt while in the hypnotic state.

Nevertheless, writes Charles Harris, the knowledge is truly in his mind, and shows itself in unmistakable ways, especially by causing him to perform or to refrain from performing actions, which but for the possession of this knowledge, he would not have per-

formed or refrained from performing. What is still more extraordinary, a sensitive hypnotic subject may be made both to see and not to see the same object at the same moment. For example, he may be told not to see a lamp-post, whereupon he becomes (in the ordinary sense) quite unable to see it. Nevertheless, he does see it, because he avoids it, and cannot be induced by any device to precipitate himself against it.

In the unique case of God incarnate therefore, we may at least reasonably suppose that our Lord's divine knowledge, while still personally possessed by Him as God, was deliberately kept below the threshold of His human consciousness, but could be drawn upon as and when His Father gave to Him to know, as Man, what eternally He knew as God. (see Jn viii. 47, xiv. 10, 24).[4]

- **Objection** – The objection is sometimes raised, 'If Jesus was God, how can we say that He died?'

Answer: We have to say something like 'God died' because of *1 Corinthians 2:8* which speaks of the rulers who had *crucified the Lord of glory.*

Seeing that Jesus was the God-Man, would we find it strange to read that it was God's blood which was shed for us? In fact, this is the very thing that Scripture says: *'Be shepherds of the church of God, which he bought with his own blood.' – Acts 20:28.*

Nevertheless, we need to explain further what Paul, and we ourselves, mean by saying something like that. What can those, who seem to feel victorious in asking questions like this, think about the other side of the coin? An example is found when we read an instance such as that described in *Mark 5:25-34,* where a woman who had been subject to bleeding for twelve years had faith to believe that if she just touched the garments of Jesus she would be healed – so she did this. *Verse 30* says:

> *At once Jesus realised that power had gone out from him. He turned around in the crowd and asked, 'Who touched my clothes?'*

Is it normal for someone, who is just a human, to have power go out from them for healing?

Similarly, *Luke 6:19* says: *and the people all tried to touch him, because power was coming from him and healing them all.*

There is no doubt that Jesus was both God and man. Remember that *Colossians 2:9* states, *For in Christ all the fullness of the Deity lives in bodily form.* In *John 2:19-22* He stated that He would raise Himself from the dead in three days. How could a dead man, someone who was just a man, possibly raise himself from the dead? Jesus was not just a man! I can't believe for a moment that anyone who believes in the true God would suggest that God could die. The answer to the alleged problem is that it was the God-Man who died, not God. In other words, when Jesus of Nazareth died there was no more a living God-Man. The God-Man suffered all the excruciating agony of crucifixion. He suffered right up to the point of death. God knows what it is like to die but *divinity* did not die. Someone coined the phrase, 'As in the womb, so in the tomb.' The divine Word was quiescent in the womb of Mary and was likewise inactive in the tomb for three days. Awareness of His deity had generally been kept below the threshold of the consciousness of Jesus. His divinity only flashed through His humanity in exceptional circumstances. The God-Man could only live again by resurrection from the dead. After three days, the divinity of the God-Man caused Him to awaken from death. This could not happen from the standpoint of His humanity. His divinity must break the bonds of death. He could not die as God and He could not rise from the dead as man. Why did God become man? Robert G. Gromacki answers our question:

If Jesus had been born through natural generation, He would have died like all mortals, but His death would not have had an infinite, eternal redemptive value. There had to be the incarnation of God the Son through the virgin conception to bring together into one person the two features necessary for redemption: human mortality and divine value.[5]

Gromacki affirms what **Hebrews 2:14, 15** declares:
Since the children have flesh and blood, he too shared in their humanity so that by his death he might destroy him who holds the power of death – that is, the devil – and free those who all their lives were held in slavery by their fear of death.

Praise God the whole of humanity can benefit from this marvellous situation. As we individually accept the salvation made possible because of the death of the God-Man, which was of infinite value – sufficient to substitute for the debt of sinfulness of everyone who has ever lived, we are declared justified. That is, declared free from condemnation. We are all sinners and deserve to die as the penalty for our sin. As we accept Jesus as our Saviour His death stands in place of ours. We go free. Why not enjoy again the reading of **John 3:16,** the best known verse in the Bible?

'For God so loved the world that he gave his one and only Son, that whoever believes in him shall not perish but have eternal life.'

What a wonderful Saviour! What marvellous grace! What a glorious prospect for all sinners willing to repent!

Before moving from this section I think it would be helpful for Jehovah's Witnesses if I clarify a little more what Jesus did for us in dying for us. They have a very inadequate view of the Atonement, claiming that Jesus' perfect life was offered as a corresponding ransom for Adam's perfect life which was forfeited. I will let Scripture speak for itself and just quote a few verses.

Romans 8:3, 4   Jesus was a *'sin offering'*.

1 Corinthians 15:3   *'Christ died for our sins.'* Please note that it was not just a corresponding ransom for Adam's sin as the Watchtower asserts.

2 Corinthians 5:21   He was made *'to be sin for us'*.

Galatians 3:13   *'Christ redeemed us from the curse of the law.'*

1 Timothy 2:6   *'The man Christ Jesus, who gave himself as a ransom for all men.'*

Hebrews 2:9   *'Suffered death, so that by the grace of God he might taste death for everyone.'*

1 Peter 2:24   *'He himself bore our sins in his body on the tree.'*

I leave it to my readers to decide whether any ordinary man, even a perfect man, could provide what Jesus offered for us.

● **Objection** – *1 Corinthians 15:24-28* says:
Then the end will come, when he hands over the kingdom to God the Father after he has destroyed all

dominion, authority and power. For he must reign until he has put all his enemies under his feet. The last enemy to be destroyed is death. For he 'has put everything under his feet.' Now when it says that 'everything' has been put under him, it is clear that this does not include God himself, who put everything under Christ. When he has done this, then the Son himself will be made subject to him who put everything under him, so that God may be all in all.

This verse shows clearly that Jesus is not God but rather that He is subject to Him.

Answer: Quite clearly this passage has to do with the work of Christ in the plan of redemption. It has nothing whatever to do with the nature of Christ. The objectors have their critical eyes on the handing over of the kingdom to the Father; and the Son subjecting Himself to the Father. We need to have a close look at what is being said here.

The kingdom is to be handed over *'after he has destroyed all dominion, authority and power'*. Satan and his demons and the occupants of this planet have been in rebellion against God. *'He must reign until he has put all his enemies under his feet. The last enemy to be destroyed is death.'* We have here an obvious messianic reference based upon **Psalm 110:1.** The reign being referred to extends from the Second Advent to the end of the millennium. This must be so, for Satan is an enemy to be put under His feet and he is not destroyed until then – **Revelation 20:10.** *'The last enemy to be destroyed is death.'* **Revelation 20:14.** Death, too, is to be destroyed at the end of the millennium. It was God's intention that man should have dominion over the Earth – that all things were to be under his feet. Speaking of man **Psalm 8:6** says:

You made him ruler over the works of your hands; you put everything under his feet.

Because of the Fall, this purpose of God has been realized only in the Messiah. The Messiah (Jesus) is to be King over the Earth and is to restore His dominion to the state God originally intended. When the plan of redemption is complete there will be the Kingdom of the World under the Messiah and the Universal Kingdom of God. The next step is a logical one, the Messiah will subject Himself, as King of the restored Earth, to God. *When he has done this, then the Son himself will be made subject to him who put everything under him, so that God may be all in all.* Paul is here reiterating what he said in *verse 24.* When Christ, as King of the restored world, returns it in perfection to God, *'God may be all in all.'*

It is clear that what we have read has to do with Christ in His *position* adopted for the purposes of the plan of redemption. It has nothing, not even a little bit, to do with His *nature!*

Let us think a little more on the situation. Is Christ in rebellion against God? Obviously not! The Christ of the Bible is portrayed as always being in subjection to God *now!* Surely it will be obvious that the subjection of *verse 28* is something quite different from normal personal subjection. The context makes it clear that Paul is speaking of the concluding events of the plan of redemption. I must emphasize that the subjection spoken of is not the normal subjection of Christ but is something for the future. The subjection is referring to the handing over of the Kingdom, by the Messiah, to God. Everything is back to what God intended it to be, then God will be all in all.

- Objection – *Colossians 1:15* says that Jesus is the 'first-born' of creation. This means that He was the first creature created. How then can it be said that He was the Creator?

Answer: It is hardly believable, but nevertheless true, that some (such as Jehovah's Witnesses) pick out a few words in the midst of the wonderful statements about Jesus in *Colossians chapter 1* and try and claim by them that Jesus was created. The words are from *verse 15: the first-born over all creation.*

First of all, let it be said, one cannot be born and created at the same time. It is also sadly true that those who twist Scripture in this way are heaping condemnation upon themselves. To take this text out of context, as is done by those trying to find evidence for Jesus being but a creature, is to make Holy Writ appear to be wholly rot. It has been well said, *'A text taken out of context is but a pretext.'*

Had it been Paul's wish to say that Christ was 'first-created', he had the word *protoktistos* available. But neither Paul nor any other Bible writer uses this word with reference to Christ.

It must be emphasized again that we cannot hope to understand the Bible unless we determine what the terminology used meant to the people of the time in which the particular book was written. It is an incontrovertible fact that the term *'firstborn',* as used in the Bible, does not necessarily identify one physically born first. The natural first-born in a family was entitled to certain rights and privileges which gave him the chief position among the offspring of the family – a position of honour and dignity. This figure was often transferred to other people and things to indicate their pre-eminent position. The following are some examples:

Yahweh said of His chosen nation, *'Israel is my firstborn son'* – **Exodus 4:22.**

He also calls the tribe of Ephraim *'My firstborn son'* – **Jeremiah 31:9.**

David was raised to the pre-eminent position *'the most exalted of the kings of the earth'* and, consequently, Yahweh appoints him to be His *'firstborn'* – **Psalm 89:27.**

Speaking of Job, Bildad the Shuhite said, *'Death's firstborn devours his limbs'* – **Job 18:13.** Evidently, this was the description of a disease considered to be the chief among the fatal maladies.

Quite positively, these examples of the Bible usage of the term *'firstborn'* cannot be taken literally. Surely we must accept that in the context of **Colossians 1** it means that Jesus holds the pre-eminent position over all creation? If we read the passage with unbiased eyes it is not difficult to see that Paul called Jesus *'the firstborn'* because *'by him all things were created'*. Is it not obvious that as Creator, Jesus must have the pre-eminent position over all creatures? Jesus is not called *'the firstborn'* because He was created first but because He created all things. *The New English Bible* gives a clear picture of what Paul intended to convey:

Colossians 1:15 *His is the primacy over all created things.*

We need only to examine some following statements in **verse 18** to see that the theme Paul is pursuing is the *pre-eminence* of Jesus.

He is the head of the body, the church

He is the beginning and the firstborn from among the dead

Why is Paul relating all these things in this passage of

Scripture? He wanted those influenced by the Gnostics of his day to understand:

That in everything he might have the supremacy.

Christ is Lord of creation – Lord of His Church – Lord of the dead. Pre-eminence is the theme Paul is pursuing. He is demonstrating the absolute supremacy of Christ in every sphere. How incongruous it is to try to insist that in the middle of it all he asserts that our Lord is merely a creature.

Paul is saying, What of you? What do you think of Christ? Have you surrendered to Him that He may have the supremacy in your life?

*Christ is not valued at all unless He be valued above all – **Augustine**.*

- **Objection** – ***Revelation 3:14*** states that Jesus was the beginning of the creation of God. How can it be denied that He was created?

Answer: Some modern translations still render the section of this verse under review as: *The Beginning of the creation of God* – New American Standard Bible.

However, it has a footnote to *'Beginning'* which says *'origin or source'*. Here, then, is the answer to those who try to claim that here we have evidence that Jesus was created. The Greek word translated *'beginning'* is *arche*. A. T. Robertson wrote:

The beginning of the creation of God (HE ARCHE TES KTISEOS TOU THEOU). Not the first of creatures as the Arians held and Unitarians do now, but the originating source of creation through whom God works.[6]

A whole string of translations could be offered but I will offer only The New International Version and The New Revised Standard Version:

the ruler of God's creation – NIV
the origin of God's creation – NRSV

- **Objection** – *Proverbs 8:22 'The LORD brought me forth as the first of his works, before his deeds of old.'* This verse is really speaking of Jesus and it shows that He was created. (See Bible footnote to this passage.)

Answer: Is this verse saying that *wisdom* was literally created and that it is Jesus Christ being spoken of?

If *wisdom* was literally created then we arrive at the difficult situation of there being a time when God was without wisdom. Obviously, this cannot be what is intended. I do not deny that God's wisdom had personal existence in Jesus, or that He possessed the fullness of God's wisdom, but I do deny that all of God's wisdom was encapsulated in Him. What I mean to say is that God's wisdom did not exist only in Jesus (the Son). No doubt the purpose of the Proverb is to emphasize the value of wisdom – wisdom is older than creation and is recommended to us.

It is true that some translations have *'created'* where the NIV footnote has *'brought me forth'*. The idea behind the expression is that God used wisdom in carrying out His works. Translations such as the NASB render it as follows:

'The LORD possessed me at the beginning of His way, before His works of old.'

Derek Kidner is well worth considering on what the Proverb is really saying:

*The Arians (who denied the deity of Christ) appealed to LXX's 'created', to prove that Christ, the Wisdom of God, was not eternal. But our concern must be with the word's normal meaning, and with the general sense of the passage. Elsewhere this verb (**qana**) pre-*

dominantly means 'get', and hence 'possess' (see eg., Pr. 4:5, 7, where wisdom is the object as here). Of its 84 Old Testament occurrences, only six or seven allow the sense 'create' (Gn. 14:19, 22; Ex. 15:16; Dt. 32:6; Pss. 74:2; 139:13; Pr. 8:22), and even these do not require it. The derived nouns still more strongly emphasize possession.[7]

To suggest that there was a time when God lacked wisdom and that He had to create it is absurd and we will spend no more time or space on the suggestion.

- **Objection** – *John 3:16* reports that Jesus was God's 'only begotten' Son, so how can it be denied that He was created?

Answer: The answer to this question involves a discussion of the Greek word *monogenes* which was translated in the Authorized King James Version as 'only begotten'.

The translation of this word as *'only begotten'* has caused many to understand that Jesus was brought into existence at some time in the distant past. *'Therefore,'* they say, *'He cannot be the eternal God.'* Their confidence in some of the older translations which translate *monogenes* as *'Only-begotten'* is misplaced. Greek Scholars are better informed today and modern translations have corrected this wrong rendition of *monogenes.*

Mono obviously means something like *'one'*, however, *genes* is not derived from *gennao*, to beget, but from *genos*, a kind or class. Therefore, *monogenes* should be translated something like *unique*. This is the meaning that modern translations provide. An example is the rendering of *John 1:18* in the New International Version: *No one has ever seen God, but God the One and Only, who is at the Father's side, has made him known.*

It is interesting to read ***Hebrews 11:17*** where Isaac is referred to as the *monogenes* son of Abraham. Of course Isaac was not the only son of Abraham; neither was he his eldest son. Here again the thought should be expressed something like *'the unique son', or 'only son'.*

The King James Version has ***Psalm 22:20*** saying: *Deliver my soul from the sword; my darling from the power of the dog.*

The Septuagint Version (LXX) translates *'darling'* (Hebrew *yechida)* of this verse as *monogenes.* The idea of someone special, unique, comes shining through. The same thing applies to the Hebrew word *yechida* (darling) in ***Psalm 35:17.***

I think I can safely say that the best discussion of this word is found in an article 'God's Only Son,' in the *Journal of Biblical Literature,* Vol. LXX11, December 1953, by Dale Moody. One vital point of clarification that Moody makes is succinctly stated in *The International Standard Bible Encyclopedia.*[8]

> *The Old Latin MSS rendered **monogenes** by Lat. **Unicus** ('only') rather than **unigenitus** ('only begotten'). In the Vulgate Jerome changed **unicus** to **unigenitus** ('only begotten') for theological reasons, ie., to ensure the doctrine that Jesus was 'begotten, not made.' (In passages that lack this theological interest (**Lk. 7:12; 8:42; 9:38**) he kept **unicus** as the translation of Gk. **Monogenes**.) The Vulgate exercised a formidable influence on the AV and subsequent English translations.*

Do not let this point escape you – the words *'only begotten'* do not rightly belong in the English translation! They only found a place there because of the tampering of Jerome with the facts and the apparent willingness of some subsequent scholars to follow in his footsteps. It has been suggested that they do this for theological rather than linguistic reasons.

Jesus was not begotten, neither was He created. Many who say Jesus was a literal Son of God make claims for one or more of these ways He is said to have come into being. If people want to follow this line of literalness they should explain how it is possible to be absolutely literal when there was no mother. The terms Father and Son, when related to Jesus, can hardly be literal really. To insist upon taking them literally is to impose upon these terms twenty-first century concepts which did not necessarily apply in the ancient Near East where the Bible was written. The Father-Son relationships in the Godhead should be understood in a metaphorical sense, not in a literal sense.

Conclusion

So much for the usual objections raised against the deity of Jesus Christ. In some areas we must be content to try to solve problems to the best of our ability. Our answers, though, must be faithful to what is clearly revealed in Scripture. In most areas of investigation we necessarily work from the clear to the unclear. What appears above is a sincere attempt to follow in that direction. We must appreciate that during the plan of redemption Jesus plays many roles. Perhaps they are all summed up best in the description of Him as Mediator. From beginning to end He represents God and works on our behalf.

The New Testament writers, under inspiration, sometimes referred to Jesus from the perspective of His deity, and sometimes from the perspective of His humanity. They saw no contradiction in doing this and neither should we because there is none – Jesus was the God-Man.

Those who wish to throw up a few objections need to stop and take stock of their position. They need to take notice of all the positive evidence for the deity of Jesus such as presented above. If they insist on maintaining their negative stance as opposers of His deity, they need to be able to answer all of what has been presented above. I am able to say that they can't because I have sat where the objectors sit and I know very well that an honest investigation of the biblical evidence shows very clearly that Christ is God. E. Calvin Beisner was able to claim:

> *Were there no passages at all which directly call Christ God, we would still have a great weight of evidence that that is the New Testament conception of him, for in all senses he is depicted as precisely parallel to God the Father.*[9]

[1] B. B. Warfield, *Biblical and Theological Studies,* The Presbyterian and Reformed Publishing Company, Philadelphia, Pennsylvania, 1952, page 60.

[2] Ibid, pages 62, 63.

[3] I. Howard Marshall, *Eschatology and the New Testament,* Ed. W. Hullit Gloer, Hendrickson Publishers, Peabody, Mass. 1988, page 133.

[4] Alan N. Stibbs, *God Became Man,* London: The Tyndale Press, 1957, pages 11-14.

[5] Robert G. Gromacki, *The Virgin Birth: Doctrine of Deity,* Baker Book House, Grand Rapids, Michigan, 1981, page 134.

[6] A. T. Robertson, *Word Pictures in the New Testament,* Harper and Bros. Ltd. NY, 1932, Vol. VI, page 321.

[7] Derek Kidner, *Proverbs,* The Tyndale Press, London, 1964, page 79.

[8] *The International Standard Bible Encyclopedia,* Wm. B. Eerdmans Publishing Company, Grand Rapids, Michigan, 1986, Vol. 3, page 606.

[9] E. Calvin Beisner, *God In Three Persons,* Living Studies, Tyndale House Publishers, Inc. Wheaton, Illinois, 1984, page 33.

Chapter 10

The Holy Spirit in the Old Testament

While there is a good deal of information about the Holy Spirit in Scripture we don't learn anywhere near as much about Him as we do about Jesus. This is to be expected really because the Bible is very much about Jesus. As He said in *John 5:39:*

> *'You diligently study the Scriptures because you think that by them you possess eternal life. These are the Scriptures that testify about me.'*

It should be clear to all that the indispensable requirement for the well-being of the Universe is the vindication of God. This comes about primarily because of God's love, grace, and mercy exhibited in His programme for the redemption of this planet and its inhabitants. Here, as any student of Scripture should know, Jesus is at the forefront.

What I have related above is generally true but, interestingly, it is not quite true as far as the Old Testament is concerned. There we have some indicators of both the personality and the deity of the Holy Spirit but not much that would indicate who and what the Word is. It is important to understand, too, that the Hebrew word for *spirit* can also mean 'wind', and 'breath'. Hence there are dangers in using the proof-text approach in the Old Testament to 'prove' the Holy Spirit. A knowledge of Hebrew is vital in interpreting the meaning of the word for spirit from its context.

I want to inject the thought here that, as it was the Holy Spirit who inspired the men of old to write God's Book, He is also very much needed by us in our effort to understand it. We need to pray that the Holy Spirit will guide and bless us in all our research.

> *Come, Holy Ghost, for moved by Thee*
> *The prophets wrote and spoke;*
> *Unlock the truth, Thyself the key,*
> *Unseal the sacred Book.*

The Holy Spirit was involved with creating

Genesis 1:2 *Now the earth was formless and empty, darkness was over the surface of the deep, and the Spirit of God was hovering over the waters.*

Job 33:4 *The Spirit of God has made me.*

Psalm 104:30 *When you send your Spirit, they are created.*

We are not left in doubt that the Holy Spirit was involved in Creation. We will see later that the Three members of the Trinity were all involved.

The personality of the Holy Spirit as represented in the Old Testament

2 Samuel 23:2 *'The Spirit of the LORD spoke through me.'*

1 Kings 22:24 *'Which way did the spirit from the LORD go when he went from me to speak to you?'*

Isaiah 63:10 *Yet they rebelled and grieved his Holy Spirit.*

Micah 2:7 *'Is the Spirit of the LORD angry? Does he do such things?'*

Although many references to the Holy Spirit indicate only His powerful acts and are written therefore in an impersonal way, these must be understood in the light of the complete revelation that the Holy Spirit is a Person. This revelation comes more clearly to light in the New Testament, as we shall shortly observe. But first let us note that revelation from God is progressive:

Romans 16:25, 26 *Now to him who is able to establish you by my gospel and the proclamation of Jesus Christ, according to the revelation of the mystery hidden for long ages past, but now revealed and made known through the prophetic writings by the command of the eternal God, so that all nations might believe and obey him.*

Ephesians 3:4-6 *The mystery of Christ, which was not made known to men in other generations as it has now been revealed by the Spirit of God's holy apostles and prophets. This mystery is that through the gospel the Gentiles are heirs together with Israel, members together of one body, and sharers together in the promise in Christ Jesus.*

The fact that revelation from God is progressive should be self-evident. Hence we learn far more about the personality of the Holy Spirit and the Word in the New Testament than in the Old. Who can doubt that, as time went by, more and more information about God and His plans was revealed to His people? A classic example relates to the Word. The Old Testament hardly indicates that He is a person. Yet there are some hints:

Psalm 33:6 *By the word of the LORD were the heavens made.*

When we come to the New Testament, John launches straight in and tells us that the Word was already there when all things began, that He was with God and was God also. Not only that, but that He created everything. More yet! He was incarnated! – *John 1:1–14.*

We move then to a study of the New Testament evidence which reveals the personality and deity of the Holy Spirit.

Chapter 11

The Holy Spirit in the New Testament

The Holy Spirit is a person
The Holy Spirit is contrasted with wicked spirits

Please read *1 Timothy 4:1* and *Mark 3:20-30 now,* especially *verses 29* and *30*. Humans can submit either to the Holy Spirit or to wicked spirits. This clearly implies His personality, for the wicked spirits are persons.

The Holy Spirit performs personal actions in association with other persons

Matthew 28:19 Jesus' baptismal formula requires that converts be baptized in the 'name' (the three are included in the single 'name') of the Father, the Son, and the Holy Spirit. Some claim that the Holy Spirit is merely an influence which proceeds from the Father. If this were true, it would surely be superfluous to include the Holy Spirit in the formula!

Acts 15:28 It seemed good to the Holy Spirit and to us

not to burden you with anything beyond the following requirements.

Can an impersonal force regard something as 'good'? Both parties regarded their decision as good. Both parties were persons.

> ***Revelation 22:17** The Spirit and the bride say, 'Come!' And let him who hears say, 'Come!'*

Any argument that the Holy Spirit is not a Person cannot stand in the light of the fact that He is spoken of as offering an invitation in company with other persons.

The Holy Spirit takes the place of Jesus

He is the *'Counsellor'* of ***John 14:16.*** The Holy Spirit was to take the place of Jesus. How could an impersonal force take the place of the divine Jesus on Earth? I will have a lot more to say on this verse in the next chapter when we consider some objections to the personality and deity of the Holy Spirit.

The Holy Spirit exhibits qualities that evidence personal existence

In the interests of conserving space, I must ask you to examine closely the evidence which follows directly from the Bible. The Holy Spirit has the following qualities possessed only by persons:

Has intelligence, teaches, testifies	***John 14:26; 15:26; Luke 12:12; 1 Corinthians 2:13***
Lives with people	***John 14:17***
Guides, speaks, prophesies, glorifies	***John 16:13, 14***
Witnesses	***Acts 5:32***

Speaks	*Acts 8:29; 10:19, 20; 28:25; Hebrews 3:7*
Sets people apart for service	*Acts 13:2*
Sends people on their way	*Acts 13:4*
Commands and forbids	*Acts 8:29; 16:6, 7*
Intercedes	*Romans 8:26*
Works miracles	*Acts 2:4; 8:39*
Loves	*Romans 15:30*
Has a mind	*Romans 8:27*
Has a will	*1 Corinthians 12:11*
Appoints	*Acts 20:28.*
Can be vexed and grieved	*Ephesians 4:30;* compare *Isaiah 63:10*
Can be insulted	*Hebrews 10:29*
Can be lied to	*Acts 5:3*

I haven't mentioned 'fellowship' above because I wish to give it some attention. *1 John 1:3* says: *Our fellowship is with the Father and with his Son, Jesus Christ.* (The word for fellowship here is *koinonia.*)

2 Corinthians 13:14 says: *The fellowship of the Holy Spirit be with you all.* (The word for fellowship is *koinonia* here too.)

Our ability to have fellowship with the Father and the Son exists because they are Persons. Surely, the same thing must be said in our fellowship with the Holy Spirit. How could we possibly have fellowship with something like the wind? (The analogy often offered by those who say the Spirit is just a force from God.)

We could hardly wish for a greater body of evidence which reveals that the Holy Spirit is a Person than we have offered above.

The Holy Spirit is God

It would be expected that those who accept that the Holy Spirit is a force from God would have very little trouble in taking the next step of accepting that He is part of the Godhead once they recognize Him to be a Person. Others who think that He and Jesus are the same Person aren't bothered with the question until they realize that He is a separate Person. The Arians thought that the Holy Spirit was a person but that He was created by the Son.[1]

We shall now see more clearly that the Holy Spirit is God.

The Holy Spirit is clearly referred to as God

Acts 5:3, 4 Then Peter said, 'Ananias, how is it that Satan has so filled your heart that you have lied to the Holy Spirit and have kept for yourself some of the money you received for the land? Didn't it belong to you before it was sold? And after it was sold, wasn't the money at your disposal? What made you think of doing such a thing? You have not lied to men but to God.'

There it is! Lying to the Holy Spirit is lying to God. The Holy Spirit is God.

Now, for comparison we will line up three passages from *Corinthians:*

*Don't you know that **you yourselves are God's temple** and that God's Spirit lives in you? If anyone destroys God's temple, God will destroy him; for God's temple is sacred, and you are that temple. 1 Corinthians 3:16, 17.*

*Do you not know that **your body is a temple of the***

Holy Spirit, *who is in you, whom you have received from God?* **1 Corinthians 6:19.**

We are the temple of the living God. 2 Corinthians 6:16. (The emphasis has been supplied in each case).

To speak of the Holy Spirit is to speak of God.

1 Corinthians 12:11 states clearly that it is the Holy Spirit who dispenses spiritual gifts. *He gives them to each one, just as he determines.* In **verse 28** of the same chapter we are told that it is God who does this. The Holy Spirit is God!

The Holy Spirit is said to be Eternal – **Hebrews 9:14.** How many Eternals are there? The Holy Spirit is the Eternal God.

The Holy Spirit can be blasphemed: *'Blasphemy against the Spirit will not be forgiven.'* **Matthew 12:31.** Blasphemy is something which can only be committed against God. The Holy Spirit is God.

The Holy Spirit is Yahweh

Please read the following verses carefully and you will see that, in the two instances mentioned, God is said to have said something but elsewhere the Holy Spirit is identified as the speaker.

The voice of the Lord **Isaiah 6:8-10**	*The Holy Spirit spoke* **Acts 28:25-28.**
The Spirit of the Lord spoke **2 Samuel 23:2**	*The God of Israel spoke* **2 Samuel 23:3.**

We must conclude that the Holy Spirit is Yahweh.

The Holy Spirit is Omniscient, Omnipresent, and Omnipotent

Omniscient: *1 Corinthians 2:10, 11 But God has revealed it to us by his Spirit. The Spirit searches all things, even the deep things of God. For who among men knows the thoughts of a man except the man's spirit within him? In the same way no-one knows the thoughts of God except the Spirit of God.*

Omnipresent: *Psalm 139:7 Where can I go from your Spirit? Where can I flee from your presence?*

Omnipotent: Romans 15:19 *By the power of signs and miracles, through the power of the Spirit.*

See also *Psalm 104:30; Zechariah 4:6; 1 Corinthians 12:11.*

There can be no doubt that the New Testament brought with it new dimensions in the understanding of the Holy Spirit. It is evident that the Christians of the Apostolic age were occupied with their relationship to the Spirit in the work that was to be done in the spreading of the Gospel rather than with setting down any statements concerning the personality and deity of the Holy Spirit. Despite this fact we find very clear evidence of their accepting that He is a Person of the Godhead.

We praise and thank the Holy Spirit for dwelling with us and in us. We love our wonderful Counsellor Friend and hope to learn more of Him in eternity. We turn now to some of the objections often raised to what we have discovered.

---

[1] George Smeaton, *The Doctrine of the Holy Spirit*, The Banner of Truth, London, 1961, pages 271, 272.

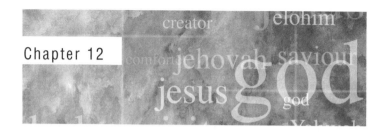

Chapter 12

Answers to objections to the personality and deity of the Holy Spirit

- **Objection** – The word spirit (Greek – *pneuma*) is also translated in the Bible as 'wind'. Therefore the Holy Spirit is just God's active force.

Answer: The conclusion drawn is not necessarily true, otherwise we would have to say that God is only an impersonal active force. *John 4:24* says *'God is spirit',* and there are also wicked spirits and these too are persons. Obviously, if we want to take away the personality of the Holy Spirit it cannot be on the basis of the word *pneuma*. The Holy Spirit is not just some power – in fact many references distinguish Him from His power. *1 Corinthians 12* distinguishes between the Holy Spirit and the gifts He distributes. *Verse 11* says, *All these are the work of one and the same Spirit, and he gives them to each one, just as he determines.* Many of the gifts of the Spirit are spoken of just prior to this verse. *Luke 1:35; 4:14; Acts 10:38; Romans 15:13, 19* and *1 Corinthians 2:4* all distinguish the power of the Holy Spirit from the Spirit Himself. Notice one of these as an example:

Acts 10:38 How God anointed Jesus of Nazareth with the Holy Spirit and power.

- **Objection** – There are references where the Holy Spirit appears to be referred to as a person but these are just examples of personification.

  Answer: Arthur W. Wainwright responds to this rather weak assertion:

  If these examples had been few in number, they could have been dismissed as metaphorical. But since they come from different authors, and are comparatively numerous, they cannot lightly be pushed aside.[1]

- **Objection** – The question is asked, 'If the Holy Spirit is a person what is His name?'

  Answer: The answer is that His name is 'The Holy Spirit'. It is just as proper for Him to be called The Holy Spirit as it is for Jesus to be called Christ (the anointed One). The evil one is called the devil (slanderer) or Satan (Adversary). These terms became names. One reason that He would be called the Holy Spirit is because of His heavenly nature in contrast with the other spirits endeavouring to influence men.

- **Objection** – *Acts 2:17* has God saying, *'I will pour out my spirit on all people.'* How could a Person be poured out?

  Answer: First of all, let us remember that the Holy Spirit is not like any person that we know. His nature is really unknown to us. We must be careful, therefore, not to place too much trust in our own reasoning on what we think may or may not be done with the Person of the Holy Spirit. We might just as well ask, 'How can we be *baptized into*

110

*Christ?' O*r, 'How can we be clothed *with Christ?' – See* **Galatians 3:27** and compare **Romans 6:3.** We must be careful not to try to press terms like this into an absolute, literal meaning. Pouring out can denote richness and abundance. See **Hosea 5:10; Psalm 45:2; Romans 5:5.** The verb concerned in **Acts 2:17** is *ekcheo.* Arndt and Gingrich say of this verb that it is used figuratively of the Holy Spirit and that *'generally whatever comes from above is connected with this verb.'*[2]

It is surely not hard to see that 'pouring out' has reference to the greater abundance and richness of the Holy Spirit's gifts that will be available at a point in time.

- **Objection** – If the Holy Spirit is a Person how could He come on Jesus as a dove *(Matthew 3:16)* and upon the disciples as tongues of fire? *(Acts 2:3).*

   Answer: Please note that 'like' and 'seemed to be' are used to describe the situation. The Spirit descended *'like a dove'* and *'what seemed to be tongues of fire'.* The phenomena we have read of were evidently visible manifestations suited to the understanding of men. It is interesting to note that **Deuteronomy 4:24** and **Hebrews 12:29** both say that God is a *'consuming fire'.* This also is only a figure of speech suited to our understanding. We can also remember that God actually led the children of Israel in their wanderings, after leaving Egypt, as a pillar of fire and as a cloud. Also, recall that His presence in the Sanctuary was manifested through the Shekinah glory.

- **Objection** – *Acts 1:5; Matthew 3:11* say that Jesus was to baptize His followers with the Holy Spirit. How can men be baptized in a Person?

   Answer: Portions of all of the above answers also apply

here. It seems that being baptized in the Spirit means for a believer to come into the sphere of the Spirit; to be immersed in His influence.

● **Objection** – *2 Corinthians 3:17 the Lord is the Spirit.*
The context shows that Jesus is the Holy Spirit. They are the same person. In other words, Jesus is the Holy Spirit.

Answer: This claim is without foundation, but seeing that it seems to have confused many I will give it considerable attention.

First of all *2 Corinthians 3:17* is certainly far from conclusive. 'The Spirit' is very likely the subject of the sentence and 'the Lord' the predicate. The sentence would then read 'the Spirit is the Lord'. What would we have then? We would obviously have a clear reference to the deity of the Holy Spirit.

I think it is fair to say that most anti-Trinitarians do not accept that the Holy Spirit is a person. However, as we have just seen, there have ever been some who say, 'Oh, yes, he is a person but that person is Jesus.' *John chapters 14-16* completely demolish such an assertion:

'I will ask the Father, and he will give you another Counsellor.' John 14:16.

What does the word 'another' mean? *Webster's Seventh New Collegiate Dictionary* provides the following definitions:

1. *1: different or distinct from the one considered 2: some other: LATER 3: being one more in addition to one or more of the same kind: NEW*
2. *1: an additional one: one more 2: one that is different from the first or present one 3: one of a group of unspecified or indefinite things.*

When Jesus made the above statement He obviously meant that He would ask for a Counsellor other than Himself because He was going away. The Counsellor would take His place. This fact is so obvious that it hardly needs stating. However, those who urge 'the Jesus/Holy Spirit one person concept' must either be unaware of what we have observed, or do they ignore it?

Looking more closely at the Greek of the statement is just as damaging to the anti-Trinitarian case, which is really an old heresy labelled Sabellianism. Leon Morris is helpful to us here:

*In Greek there are two words for 'other': **allos** means 'another of the same kind', while **heteros** points rather to 'another of a different kind'. Thus if I ask for another book, using **allos**, I am seeking another copy of the volume in question. But if you bring me a copy of another book altogether I might complain that I didn't say **heteros**. When Jesus speaks of the Spirit as 'another Comforter' (Jn. xiv. 16) the word He uses is **allos**. The most natural interpretation of all this is that the Spirit is to be thought of as another like Jesus. As Jesus is a Person, the inference is that the Spirit is also a Person. The only catch in the reasoning is that not all Greek writers used the two words for 'other' strictly.[3]*

We have no reason to expect that John did not use correct grammar here. I have not found a case from anyone wanting to try to refute this argument.

Let us ask ourselves, was Jesus fooling us? If He and the Spirit are the same why would He try and make out that 'another' would come to take His place? Was He going to come back in disguise and keep this fact from us? I cannot accept for even a moment that the Jesus I know would act like that.

The word for 'Comforter' in the Greek is *parakletos*. It combines two words *para* – to the side of, and *kletos* – called. It means then, 'One called to the side of, to help.' Please note that it is a word always used of persons. There is no English equivalent of the word so it is translated in many different ways. But it always means someone who will be of help. So, words like Comforter, Counsellor, and Helper are often used. Advocate is another word used. Please listen to Leon Morris again:

The point of importance for us is that the word was applied to persons. However we translate it (and something like 'Helper' might be the meaning in the Johannine passage), in the first century it would be understood of a person. Certainly nobody then would have imagined that the word would denote a vague influence, a power flowing from God. Its use marks the Spirit as a Person.[4]

Quite clearly Jesus was saying that another like Him would come. It is just as clear that He did not say that He Himself would be the one that would come. In ***John 15:26*** Jesus says that He will send the Holy Spirit and that the Spirit would testify about Him (Jesus).

'When the Counsellor comes, whom I will send to you from the Father, the Spirit of truth who goes out from the Father, he will testify of me.'

It is rather upsetting when we are confronted by those who are really suggesting that Jesus was playing games with us. Please, let us accept the clarity of what we have just read.

There is another astonishing fact that we should take note of. It too has to do with the original Greek. We find that the rules of Greek grammar are deliberately broken by Jesus and John in order to show clearly that the Holy Spirit is a Person. I will let Leon Morris do some more explaining for us:

> *Now in Greek the word for 'Spirit' is neuter, and should in strict grammar be referred to as 'It'. When John uses a pronoun to refer to 'Spirit' and the two words are close together, he usually respects his grammar and uses the correct form 'It'. But if a word or two intervenes he nearly always uses the masculine form 'He'. This is grammatically incorrect, but most illuminating. The explanation is surely that John habitually thought of the Spirit in personal terms, as 'He' rather than as 'It'. Naturally enough his thinking dictated this form of speech. Where he can, he uses personal forms of the pronouns. He even does it occasionally where the pronoun and the word for Spirit occur side by side. See John xvi. 13, 'he, the Spirit of truth'.[5]*

While Morris states that it was John who broke Greek grammar, I assume that he faithfully reported what Jesus had said – so, it was Jesus who originally took the step outlined in order to emphasize that the Spirit is a Person.

> ***John 14:16, 17*** *'And I will ask the Father, and he will give you another Counsellor to be with you forever – the Spirit of truth. The world cannot accept him, because it neither sees him nor knows him. But you know him, for he lives with you and will be in you.'* *(Please read also **John 16:7, 8**).*

As we have seen, there is no problem in establishing that the Holy Spirit is distinguished from the Father and the Son. Here are some texts clearly portraying this:

Isaiah 48:16 – The Messiah is speaking: *'Come near me and listen to this: From the first announcement I have not spoken in secret; at the time it happens, I am there. And now the Sovereign LORD has sent me, with his Spirit.'* There is no doubt that we have three individuals portrayed here.

Matthew 28:19 provides the baptismal formula involving the Three – not two – or one.

Luke 3:21, 22 describes the scene at Jesus' baptism. The Holy Spirit descends upon Jesus who is being baptized and the Father speaks to Jesus from heaven. Good arithmetic confirms that there are *three* spoken of here.

John 14:16 is a text we have already reviewed but I must mention that Jesus (one Person) was going to ask the Father (a second Person) to send another Counsellor (the Holy Spirit – a third Person). Please also read *1 Corinthians 12:4-6; 2 Corinthians 13:14; Ephesians 2:18;* as other examples. (We will notice some other similar texts when we study the Trinity.)

The Holy Spirit is in the world, since Pentecost, carrying on the work of God. He represents Christ, He represents the Father. Consequently, He is called *'the Spirit of God'* – *1 Corinthians 2:11.*

'the Spirit of the living God'	*2 Corinthians 3:3*
'the Spirit of the Lord'	*2 Corinthians 3:17*
'the Spirit of glory and of God'	*1 Peter 4:14*
'the Spirit of Jesus'	*Acts 16:7*
'the Spirit of God . . . the Spirit of Christ'	*Romans 8:9*
'the Spirit of Jesus Christ'	*Philippians 1:19*
'God sent the Spirit of his Son into our hearts'	*Galations 4:6*

It would be helpful at this point if we paused to consider the word 'of' used in the phrases mentioned above.

Jesus is called *'the Son of David'*. Does this mean that He is David? Of course not! It means that David is His source, or, in other words, that He comes from David. The word 'of' must be understood as the genitive of origin. Jesus is not the Spirit but the Spirit proceeds from Jesus. I have made this statement because some have insisted that the Spirit of Jesus must be Jesus Himself. In this they have erred.

We need to review again some statements from **John chapters 14-16.**

The Holy Spirit is sent by the Father at the Son's request – **John 14:16.**

He is sent in Jesus' name – **John 14:26.**

According to **John 16:7** Jesus sends the Spirit.

Jesus sends the Spirit from the Father – **John 15:26.**

The Father and the Son are so inextricably bound up together that Jesus can say that the Holy Spirit *'will bring glory to me by taking from what is mine and making it known to you. All that belongs to the Father is mine. That is why I said the Spirit will take from what is mine and make it known to you.'* – **John 16:14, 15.**

The evidence is consistent and too obvious for us to be confused by the misinterpretation of a few texts thrown up by those who insist that Jesus and the Spirit are the same person. They are both Members of the Triune God and as such the Three (Father, Son, and Holy Spirit) are all part of the One God who acts. When one Member acts, His action has the quality of them all acting because they are the One God. When the Holy Spirit comes to us it is the same as Jesus or the Father, or both, coming to us. The Father sends the Spirit. Jesus sends the Spirit, the Spirit is the Spirit of God, He is the Spirit of the Father, He is the Spirit of Jesus, or, He is the Holy Spirit.

Before moving on, I would like to suggest a little experiment which, I believe, further demolishes any opinion that Jesus and the Holy Spirit are the same Person. Please substitute the name 'Jesus' for 'the Holy Spirit' in the following passages and see what you think. I will present the name 'Jesus' in bold italics where 'The Holy Spirit' would normally occur. This process should be acceptable if Jesus and the Holy Spirit are the same Person.

Matthew 1:20, 21   Jesus' miraculous conception and birth was due to the power of *Jesus*.

Isaiah 11:1, 2   Isaiah foretold that *Jesus* would rest on Jesus.

John 1:32, 33   John the Baptist was told to recognize Jesus when *Jesus* came upon Jesus.

Acts 10:38   says God anointed Jesus with *Jesus*.

Matthew 3:13-17   The record of *Jesus* coming upon Jesus at Jesus' baptism.

Matthew 4:1   After his baptism Jesus is led by *Jesus* into the wilderness.

Luke 4:14   Jesus returned to Galilee in the power of *Jesus*.

John 3:34   Jesus had *Jesus* without measure.

Luke 4:18   Jesus had *Jesus* on Him.

Matthew 12:28   Jesus drove out demons by *Jesus*.

Acts 2:33   When Jesus returned to the right hand of God, *Jesus* was poured out.

John 14:16   Jesus now comes to us and indwells us by His representative *Jesus*.

John 16:14   *Jesus* would glorify Jesus.

Well, what do you think? I know that Scripture is quite clear that Jesus and the Holy Spirit are separate Persons. They complement each other and are part of the Trinity but we should not be confused by those who insist that they are the same Person.

We have gone about as far as we can go for now in our endeavour to understand the nature of the Holy Spirit and how He functions in His relationship with the Father and the Son. Christians in the early centuries of the Christian era struggled to understand. Those of the Western Church said that the Spirit proceeds from the Father and the Son. The Eastern branch of the Church disagreed, saying that He proceeds from the Father only. Is there a lesson here to be learned? Which interpretation is correct? Let us be content to admit that we cannot understand more than Inspiration has chosen to reveal to us. We must be faithful to what we have been told in God's word. We must work from the clear to the unclear. We must not try to appear to be wise beyond what is revealed. If something is unclear we must be humble enough to say, 'I'm not sure about that!' In many areas of study we might like to know more – no doubt we do! Let us realize that in matters such as we are studying we are probably incapable of comprehending more anyway.

Conclusion

There may be another objection or two but none that can contradict the clear message we have discerned throughout our research. The Holy Spirit is a Person of the Trinity; He is not the Father, neither is He the Son. He is One of the co-eternal Three. How encouraging to know that God is still with us. We have not been left comfortless. God is still with us in the Person of the Holy Spirit. His purpose is not to glorify Himself but to glorify Jesus.

Thank You for doing that for us, sweet Holy Spirit!

Come Holy Spirit, heavenly Dove,
With all Thy quickening powers;
Come, shed abroad a Saviour's love,
And that shall kindle ours.

Isaac Watts

---

[1] Arthur W. Wainwright, *The Trinity in the New Testament,* S.P.C.K, London, 1962, pages 201, 202.

[2] Arndt and Gingrich, *A Greek-English Lexicon of the New Testament and Other Early Christian Literature,* The University of Chicago Press, Chicago, Illinois, 1963, page 246.

[3] Leon Morris, *Spirit of the Living God, Inter-varsity Fellowship,* London, 1961, page 36.

[4] *Ibid,* page 35.

[5] *Ibid,* page 36.

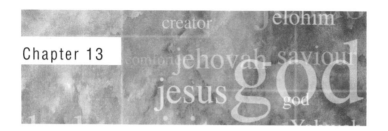

Chapter 13

Understanding the Trinity
– a final reflection

From earliest times the people of God have known Him as their Creator God in heaven. When the divine Word visited planet Earth, incarnated as Jesus of Nazareth, God's people recognized Him to be God. Yet, they knew that God was still in heaven. When Jesus returned to heaven they accepted that He had gone back to be with Father God.

When the Holy Spirit came to reside with us at Pentecost two thousand years ago, God's people recognized Him to be a Person who also was God. They never forgot, though, that God the Father and God the Son were in heaven still. While they recognized more clearly then that there were three who comprised the plurality in God, they maintained their strict monotheistic stance. They never entertained the false idea that there were three Gods. They just lived with what they understood Inspiration had revealed to them. If they had tried to proclaim that there were really three Gods they would have been met by an enormous howl of protest. But they were not interested in teaching such heresy anyway.

It was only when heretical concepts relating to the three began to be spread among them that they were forced to endeavour to make a more detailed statement of their understanding. The greatest furore requiring this arose from the teaching of Arius of Alexandria (c.256-336) who promoted the teaching that Jesus was ever only just a creature and that after He was brought into being He created the Holy Spirit. After considerable debate the early Christians formulated their understanding of the Trinity and rejected Arianism. E. Calvin Beisner states:

While we have been able to arrive fairly quickly at a New Testament doctrine of the Trinity, it did not come so easily for the early Church. A triune conception of God existed from the earliest times in the Church (we have already seen it in the New Testament), a conception in which Father, Son, and Spirit were related to as one God. But the careful formulation of this conception drawn from experience and from the teaching of Jesus and the apostles into words which could resist misinterpretation took the hard work of three centuries after the death of the last of the apostles. Such work took place in the atmosphere of constant debate, controversy, and resistance of misinterpretation and misapplication.[1]

Christians have worked very hard over the centuries to crystallize their understanding of many doctrines. There are many points on which they disagree still. Millard J. Erickson throws some valuable light on this development:

James Orr, lecturing at the end of the nineteenth century, observed that various areas of Christian doctrine had received special attention and development at different periods in the history of the church. Thus in the

second century the church dealt especially with apolo-
getics and the fundamental ideas of Christianity; in
the third and fourth centuries, with the doctrine of
God; in the early fifth century, with man and sin; in
the fifth to seventh centuries, with the person of
Christ; in the eleventh to sixteenth centuries, with the
atonement; and in the sixteenth century, with the
application of redemption (justification, etc.). There
had been doctrinal convictions, either implicit or
explicit, on these subjects previously, but it was as
crises arose in these areas at these particular periods
that the positions were more precisely articulated. Orr
suggested that the peculiar interest of the modern age
is eschatology, the one remaining undeveloped topic of
theology.[2]

M'Clintock and Strong give a brief history of the doctrine of the Trinity as held in the second and third centuries:
We call attention to the following as shedding light
upon the practice of the church during this period.
Pliny, a judge under Trajan, in the beginning of the
2nd century took the confessions of some accused
Christians, and says, 'They declared that they were to
meet on a certain day before it was light, and, among
other parts of their worship, sing a hymn to Christ as
their God.' Polycarp (ep. ad Philip. n 12) joins God
the Father and the Son together in his prayers for
grace and benediction upon men. Justin Martyr
answering, in his Second Apology, the charge of athe-
ism brought against them by the heathen, answers
'That they worshipped and adored still the God of
righteousness and his Son, as also the Holy Spirit of
prophecy.' Athenagoras answers the charge of atheism

*after the same manner. Similar testimony is afforded
by the writings of Lucian the heathen, Theophilus of
Antioch, Clemens Alexandrinus, Origen, Novatian,
and others, illustrating the practice of the Church in
paying divine honors to the Son and Holy Spirit.*[3]

Further evidences of the Trinity in the New Testament

I have already drawn attention to the baptismal formula
found in *Matthew 28:19* but for convenience sake I will
quote it again:

*Matthew 28:19 'Therefore go and make disciples of
all nations, baptizing them in the name of the Father
and of the Son and of the Holy Spirit.'*

At this point I want to draw attention to a statement by
B. B. Warfield. Warfield was a theologian of enormous
repute, very highly respected for his scholarly work. His
illumination of the implications of this verse are most
instructive. While revealing the Trinitarian teaching therein
it also shows up the amateurish attempts of the pseudo
scholars responsible for the *New World Translation* of the
Watchtower Society. They have included the name Jehovah
in their New Testament hundreds of times despite the fact
that there are thousands of manuscripts, either in whole or
in part, of the New Testament but not one of them, even
once, contains the name Jehovah. This must obviously be
condemned as adding to God's Word. Here is the rather
lengthy comment Warfield made on the baptismal formula
requiring that baptism be carried out in the name (singular)
of the Father, the Son, and the Holy Spirit:

*Fully to comprehend the implication of this mode of
statement, we must bear in mind, further, the significance of the term, 'the name,' and the associations*

laden with which it came to the recipients of this com-mission. For the Hebrew did not think of the name, as we are accustomed to do, as a mere external symbol; but rather as the adequate expression of the innermost being of its bearer. In His name the Being of God finds expression; and the Name of God – 'this glorious and fearful name, Jehovah thy God (Deut. xxviii. 58) – was accordingly a most sacred thing, being indeed virtu-ally equivalent to God Himself. It is no solecism, therefore, when we read (Isa. xxx. 27).

'Behold, the name of Jehovah cometh'; and the par-allelisms are most instructive when we read (Isa. lix. 19): 'So shall they fear the Name of Jehovah from the west, and His glory from the rising of the sun; for He shall come as a stream pent in which the Spirit of Jehovah driveth.' So pregnant was the implication of the Name, that it was possible for the term to stand absolutely, without adjunction of the name itself, as the sufficient representative of the majesty of Jehovah: it was a terrible thing to 'blaspheme the Name' (Lev. xxiv. 11). All those over whom Jehovah's Name was called were His possession to whom He owed protec-tion. It is for His Name's sake, therefore, that afflicted Judah cries to the Hope of Israel, the Saviour thereof in time of trouble: 'O Jehovah, Thou art in the midst of us, and Thy Name is called upon us; leave us not' (Jer. xiv. 9); and His people find the appropriate expression of their deepest shame in the lament, 'We have become as they over whom Thou never barest rule; as they upon whom Thy Name was not called' (Isa. lxiii. 19); while the height of joy is attained in the cry, 'Thy Name, Jehovah, God of Hosts, is called upon me' (Jer. xv. 16; cf. 11 Chron. vii. 14; Dan. ix. 18, 19).

When, therefore, Our Lord commanded His disciples to baptize those whom they brought to His obedience 'into the name of . . . ,' He was using language charged to them with high meaning. He could not have been understood otherwise than as substituting for the Name of Jehovah this other Name 'of the Father, and of the Son, and of the Holy Ghost'; and this could not possibly have meant to His disciples anything else than that Jehovah was now to be known to them by the new Name, of the Father, and the Son, and the Holy Ghost.[4]

There is also the fact that at the baptism of Jesus we find the Father speaking to Him from heaven while the Holy Spirit descended upon Him in the form of a dove:

Matthew 3:16, 17 *As soon as Jesus was baptized, he went up out of the water. At that moment heaven was opened, and he saw the Spirit of God descending like a dove and lighting on him. And a voice from heaven said, 'This is my Son, whom I love; with him I am well pleased.'*

Unmistakable threeness is seen again. We have also examined the evidence of very many references to the deity of Jesus and the Holy Spirit. I should also mention the references in other New Testament writings where the three are grouped together in an obvious Triadic pattern.

Let us consider, first, the benediction found in **2 Corinthians 13:14:** *May the grace of the Lord Jesus Christ, and the love of God, and the fellowship of the Holy Spirit be with you all.*

Here is a combined blessing conferred upon all from the three parties in association. There is an equality of status here and we cannot imagine it being acceptable if the name of someone less than God was included.

It is noteworthy that Jesus is mentioned first. When we peruse *1 Corinthians 12:4* we find the Holy Spirit being mentioned first: *There are different kinds of gifts, but the same Spirit. There are different kinds of service, but the same Lord. There are different kinds of working, but the same God works all of them in all men.*

This same order is found at *Ephesians 4:4-6.* While it is true that there is usually a priority of order in the Godhead for the purposes of the plan of redemption, it is also true that it is not rigidly adhered to and that there is no difference in worthiness no matter what order is arranged.

Other similar references linking the three Members of the Trinity can be found in *2 Thessalonians 2:13, 14; 1 Corinthians 12:4-6; Galatians 3:11-14; 4:6; 2 Corinthians 1:21, 22; 3:3; Romans 14:17, 18; 15:16-18; Philippians 3:3; Ephesians 2:11-22; 3:14-21; Titus 3:4-6; 1 Peter 1:2: 4:14; Jude 20, 21; Hebrews 6:4-6.*

---

[1] E. Calvin Beisner, *God in Three Persons*, Tyndale House Publishers, Inc. Wheaton, Illinois, 1984, pages 41, 42.

[2] Millard J. Erickson, *Contemporary Options in Eschatology*, Baker Book House, Grand Rapids, Michigan, 1977, page 11,

[3] M'Clintock and Strong, *Cyclopaedia of Biblical Theological and Ecclesiastical Literature*, New York, Harper & Bros. 1880, Vol. 10, page 553.

[4] B. B. Warfield, *Biblical and Theological Studies*, The Presbyterian and Reformed Publishing Co., Philadelphia, 1952, pages 42, 43.

Chapter 14

Answers to objections to the doctrine of the Trinity

- **Objection** – Where in Scripture is the doctrine of the Trinity clearly taught?

Answer: The doctrine of the Trinity is clearly required by Scripture but is nowhere fully explained therein. The words of some theologians are helpful to the situation:

We can know only as much concerning the inner nature of the Godhead as has been revealed to us in the Scriptures. The tri-personality of God is exclusively a truth of revelation, and one which lies outside the realm of natural reason. Its height and depth and length and breadth are immeasurable by reason of the fact that the finite is dealing with the infinite. As well might we expect to confine the ocean within – a tea cup as to place a full explanation of the nature of God within the limits of our feeble human minds.[1]

The doctrine of the Trinity lies in Scripture in solution, when it is crystallized from its solvent it does not cease to be Scriptural, but only comes into clearer view. Or, to speak without figure, the doctrine of the Trinity is given to us in Scripture, not in formulated *definition, but in fragmentary allusions; when we assembled the **disjecta membra** into their organic unity, we are not passing from Scripture, but entering more thoroughly into the meaning of Scripture. We may state the doctrine in technical terms, supplied by philosophical reflection; but the doctrine stated is a genuinely Scriptural doctrine.*

As we read the New Testament, we are not witnessing the birth of a new conception of God. What we meet within its pages is a firmly established conception of God underlying and giving its tone to the whole fabric. It is not in a text here and there that the New Testament bears its testimony to the doctrine of the Trinity. The whole book is Trinitarian to the core; all its teaching is built on the assumption of the Trinity; and its allusions to the Trinity are frequent, cursory, easy and confident. It is with a view to the cursoriness of the allusions to it in the New Testament that it has been remarked that 'the doctrine of the Trinity is not so much heard as overheard in the statements of Scripture'. It would be more exact to say that it is not so much inculcated as presupposed. The doctrine of the Trinity does not appear in the New Testament in the making, but as already made. [2]

- **Objection** – Some wonder whether we try too hard to explain God.

Answer: Surely most Christians would be quite happy to say, 'God has revealed Himself as three persons and I am content to leave it at that.' David said in the long ago, *My heart is not proud, O LORD, my eyes are not haughty; I do not concern myself with great matters or things too wonderful for me. – **Psalm 131:1.*** God is too wonderful for us to speculate about so we must be careful that we do not go beyond the bounds of what Inspiration has revealed to us. On the other hand, although we realize and accept our limitations, should we ever tire in our efforts to be able to understand our dearest Friend? Is it not true that we want to know as much about those we love as we can? Also for the sake of others, particularly those confused by the speculations of opposers, we feel the need to try to explain the doctrine in the best way we can.

- **Objection** – If we did accept that there are three Persons how can the works of one be said to be the works of the others?

Answer: In their endeavours to protect the doctrine of the Trinity, scholars have sometimes found it necessary to provide definitions that may sound, at first glance, quite bizarre. Remember that the doctrine is always under siege from aberrations which threaten it from all sides. The two which are most notorious are Modalism, the belief that God is a solitary Being who only reveals Himself in three different ways, and Tritheism, the belief that God is three separate Beings who are all one in purpose and suchlike.

The following is a definition introduced to explain the counter to these false concepts and explain, at least to some degree, the internal functions of the three:

Perichoresis is the term used in the doctrine of the Trinity to refer to the mutual interpenetration of the Persons of the godhead, so that although each person is distinct in relation to the others, nevertheless, each participates in the being of the others. The being of the Godhead is thus one and indivisible . . . . Synonyms for perichoresis are coinherence and circumincession.[3]

Millard J. Erickson acknowledges that it may have been the pseudo-Dionysius who was the first to use the term 'perichoresis' but that John of Damascus was the person who most utilized and developed it.[4] Whether the word perichoresis was in use in Augustine's day (AD354-430) is unclear. He lived at about the same time as pseudo-Dionysius. Augustine makes a brief statement that is in harmony with the definition of the word just given. He made his comment while writing of the infinity of each Person of the Trinity. He said: *So both each are in each, and all in each, and each in all, and all in all, and all are one.*[5]

To the uninitiated such statements might sound like so much gobbledegook; it is, however, a statement of truth. Millard J. Erickson provides some further clarification on what the word suggests:

> *Perichoresis means that not only do the three members of the Trinity interpenetrate one another, but all three are involved in all the works of God. While certain works are primarily or more centrally the doing of one of these rather than the others, all participate to some degree in what is done. Thus, while redemption is obviously the work of the incarnate Son, the Father and the Spirit are also involved. Similarly, sanctification is primarily the work of the Holy Spirit, but the Father and the Son are involved as well.*[6]

- **Objection** – It is objected by some that the doctrine of the Trinity is irrational.

Answer: Contrary to what many try to have us believe, the Bible is not irrational because it teaches things about God that we cannot understand. There are many things about God that are beyond our comprehension which are nevertheless accepted by Christians as being rational con-

cepts. For example, we believe that God has always existed. Also, we believe that He knows all things, even the
things that have not happened yet. Can anyone explain how
God can hear the prayers of millions of people all at the
same time? We say, *'Oh yes, but He is God!'* Quite so, and
when we find that God is a far more complex Being than we
can possibly understand, shouldn't we say the same thing?
Of course we should!

The truth is that God is what He is whether we fully
understand His nature or not. To say that we should not
accept that God is a Trinity because such a suggestion is
unreasonable is itself an unreasonable claim. The truth is
that an understanding of God is beyond human reason and
we can only get to know things about Him if He reveals
them to us. He has done this in the Holy Bible.

We reassert that despite the claim of some critics, we are
not being irrational by accepting the Trinity:

*The philosophical law of non-contradiction informs us
that something cannot be both true and false at the
same time and in the same sense. This is the fundamental law of all rational thought. And the doctrine of
the Trinity does not violate it. This can be shown by
stating first of all what the Trinity is not. The Trinity is
not the belief that God is three persons and only one
person at the same time and in the same sense. That
would be a contradiction. Rather, it is the belief that
there are three persons in one nature. This may be a
mystery, but it is not a contradiction. That is, it may go
beyond reason's ability to comprehend completely, but
it does not go against reason's ability to apprehend
consistently.*

*Further, the Trinity is not the belief that there are
three natures in one nature or three essences in one*

essence. That would be a contradiction. Rather, Christians affirm that there are three persons in one essence. This is not contradictory because it makes a distinction between person and essence.

Or, to put it in terms of the law of non-contradiction, while God is one and many at the same time, he is not one and many in the same sense. He is one in the sense of his essence but many in the sense of his persons. So there is no violation of the law of non-contradiction in the doctrine of the Trinity.[7]

- **Objection** – The Trinity doctrine is confusing.

Answer: The comments of Geisler remind us of some who seek to cause confusion by trying to make the teaching appear to be ridiculous. The real problem is that some people's minds are closed against evidence for what they do not want to believe. Dr Paley once remarked:

There is a principle which is a bar against all information, which is proof against all argument, and which cannot fail to keep a man in everlasting ignorance. This principle is contempt prior to investigation.

Here are a couple of examples:

The Jehovah's Witnesses delight in pointing out that 1+1+1=3 and not 1. This appears obvious. We certainly need no great education to be able to calculate that 1 person + 1 person + 1 person = 3 persons. However, no informed Trinitarian has ever said that 3 persons = 1 person. What Trinitarians really do say is that what we can only describe as three Persons all exist within the one Substance. The three Persons are, therefore, the One God. The threeness relates to Persons, the oneness relates to Substance. If

Trinitarians were saying that the oneness and the threeness were being used in the same sense, they surely would be contradicting themselves. But Trinitarians deny absolutely that the oneness and the threeness are being used in the same way. The oneness relates to the unity of the substance of God and the threeness relates to the Persons Who all co-exist within the one substance of God.

A Christadelphian booklet, *The Godhead Explained,* reveals similar confusion when claiming to reveal what Trinitarians believe. Of some theologians it states on page 4:

They cannot explain how one God can be also three Gods and vice versa; how God can have substance, and yet no form; or how the Son of God can, at the same time, be his own Father!

Again the confusion is only in the mind of the objector. If this was truly what Trinitarians believed it would be impossible to explain how it could be so. The truth is that it is definitely not what Trinitarians believe. I have never yet met an opponent of the Trinity who really understood what they were opposing. I confess that this was also my problem once. I have lived to regret it ever since. **Proverbs 18:13** states: *He who answers before listening – that is his folly and his shame.*

- **Objection** – Some objectors make the claim that the doctrine comes from paganism.
  Answer: The misguided attempts of some to claim that the doctrine came from paganism are without foundation. The pagans had in their religions many things which are a perversion of the truth. The Babylonians had false accounts of Creation and the Flood. This does not mean that Creation and the Flood are untrue. They had priests, temples, and

rituals, but that does not require that the priests, temples, and rituals of the true God are false either. The following is a statement which makes the true facts clear:

> *In examining the various heathen philosophies and mythologies, we find clear evidence of a belief in a certain sort of trinity, and yet something very different from the Trinity of the Bible.*[8]

The Triads of the heathen were not the same as the Bible teaches. Anyone informed on ancient Near Eastern history will know that the Egyptian Pharaoh Akhenaten believed in a single God. He has sometimes been described as the first monotheist among the pagans. Shall we say, then, that belief in a single-person God must be pagan? Endeavours to show that the Bible teaching on the Trinity is pagan are futile. Such false claims only cause confusion in the minds of the uninformed. They certainly are not methods that honour God or would be approved by Him.

- **Objection** – What of opposing views which have existed since ancient times?

  Answer: An unbalanced view leads to such errors as Tri-theism, Modalism, and Bi-theism. Tri-theism results from an overemphasis on the threeness. It results really in there being three completely separate persons or Gods. This is really Polytheism (which, really, is paganism). Modalism insists that God merely appears in three different ways, ie., as three different persons. Those who favour this heresy choose to ignore the biblical statements where the three appear together, for example at the baptism of Jesus. Bi-theism does not recognize the Holy Spirit to be a member of the Trinity and has God consisting of the Father and the Son. In order for this line of thinking to be followed, the vast amount of evidence for the personality of the Holy Spirit has to be ignored.

Some seem to take pride in proffering deviations from truth, which they may think to be exciting and new. They are seemingly unaware that what they offer is really only an ancient heresy in modern dress. At least some of such persons relish the notoriety that their newfound teaching gives to them. Many have an affinity with the Athenians mentioned in *Acts 17:21:*

(All the Athenians and the foreigners who lived there spent their time doing nothing but talking about and listening to the latest ideas.)

I want to state, with great emphasis, that for the truth on this matter to be understood, the entire evidence of the Bible must be accepted and allowed to give proper balance to conclusions arrived at. An overemphasis on one side of the light available will result in distortion. A neglect of some aspects of truth will do likewise. A few of the ancient heresies, which are resurfacing today, are as follows:

Monarchianism:
The Son, in the form of Monarchianism labelled 'Modalism', was said to be merely a mode of expression of the Father.

Sabellianism:
Sabellius, who taught that God revealed Himself in three different forms, taught a later expression of Monarchianism. In other words God played three different roles.

Arianism:

Arius taught that the Son had a beginning in that He was generated at a point in time from the Father. This error has been rejected and opposed by Christians from the beginning.

A genuine study of all that has been presented from the beginning of this essay will reveal the fact that the above suggested alternatives to the doctrine of the Trinity are not faithful to Scripture.

There is one more matter I wish to draw attention to which reveals that an understanding of Who and What God is makes other matters clearer to us.

---

[1] Lorraine Boettner, *Studies in Theology*, Presbyterian and Reformed Publishing Company, Pennsylvania, 1965, page 79.

[2] B. B. Warfield, *ibid.* pages 22 and 32.

[3] Van A. Harvey, *A Handbook of Theological Terms*, George Allen & Unwin, Ltd., London, 1966.

[4] Millard J. Erickson, *God in Three Persons*, Baker Books, Grand Rapids, Michigan, 1995, page 229.

[5] *The Nicene and Post-Nicene Fathers, St. Augustine*, Vol. iii, Wm. B. Eerdmans Publishing Co., Grand Rapids, Michigan, 1956, page 103.

[6] Millard J. Erickson, *ibid.* page 235.

[7] Norman L. Geisler, *Baker Encyclopedia of Christian Apologetics*, Baker Book House, Grand Rapids, Michigan, 1999, page 732.

[8] M'Clintock and Strong, *Cyclopedia of Biblical Theological and Ecclesiastical Literature,* New York: Harper & Bros., 1880, Vol. 10, page 556.

Chapter 15

The understanding of the Trinity available to us makes other biblical teachings clearer for us

Our understanding of the Triune nature of God helps us unquestionably to see other matters more clearly. Without this insight some matters seem decidedly to be unclear, even unacceptable to other clear teachings of Scripture. The following are prominent matters illuminated by the Christian understanding of God:

The uniqueness of Christianity

The Western World is being penetrated with Eastern religions today. Islam is strongly monotheistic, while Buddhism and Hinduism are polytheistic and pantheistic. The doctrine of the Trinity protects Christians from the inroads of these unacceptable religious systems. True Christianity and Eastern religions are quite incompatible and Christians need really to understand who the true God is in order to ensure their protection. In order to compromise with an Eastern religion one must deny the Bible teaching that God is a Trinity. The next step could be to dispose of the Bible altogether.

Deism

There are those who accept 'deism', a belief that God made us and then left us to ourselves. He went off somewhere else in the Universe. Understanding that Jesus is God helps us to appreciate how much God really loves us. He is with us and for us; He loves us so much that He came and died for us. The fact that the Holy Spirit is in the world, working on behalf of the Trinity, is a flat denial of Deism.

God is complete in Himself

God could not have been complete in Himself prior to creation unless there is a plurality of Persons in the Divine Substance. God is Love *(1 John 4:8)*. If God was just a solitary Being He would have had no opportunity to express His love until He created. But, seeing that He is a plurality of Persons, love and communication were shared in eternity between the Father, Jesus, and the Holy Spirit. God did not need to create in order to be complete, but at some point in eternity He chose to do so in order to express His love further.

The Atonement

Every human is responsible to offer God one hundred per cent righteousness. If Jesus was just a human and could only offer one hundred per cent righteousness to God there would have been no surplus for anyone else. Our confidence in His being able to save us is based on His being the Infinite God who could offer a sacrifice of infinite value. Scripture advises that He died for our sins – *1 Corinthians 15:3;* He bore our sins – *1 Peter 2:24;* He paid a ransom for all – *1 Timothy 2:6*. If Jesus was not God it seems that His sacrifice for us would be of no value for He could offer us no righteousness to cover our sinfulness.

The morality of the Atonement

Some have claimed that the biblical doctrine of the atonement is immoral. They refer to the fact that God is offended by our sin but that a third, uninvolved, innocent person has to step into the picture to pay the penalty for us. Of course, this is not the case at all. When we understand that Jesus is a Member of the Trinity we realize that there are only two parties involved. The offended God is so wonderful that He voluntarily takes the penalty upon Himself, thus becoming our Saviour.

Conclusion to our study

arrive now at the conclusion of what I have wanted to share after more than forty years of study and reflection on the subject of the Godhead. At the beginning of my religious experience I found myself studying Watchtower literature for my beliefs and as a consequence I believed that God was a solitary Being whose name was Jehovah. I believed that Jesus was merely a creature of God who obediently came to Earth to die on the part of mankind. The Holy Spirit was only a force from God, similar to the wind. After I released myself from Watchtower bondage and learned of God directly from the Bible, I found that I must believe in the Trinity of three Persons – Father, Son, and Holy Spirit. I rejoice in the knowledge and relationship I have with the Heavenly Trio today.

John 3:16 did not have the appeal to me in the past that it has today. Many have shared the thought with me that we hardly had the ultimate expression of love on the part of God if He merely sent a creature to pay the penalty for our sins. When we realize the connectedness and interpenetration of the Persons of the Trinity we cannot but appreciate with heartfelt gratitude that not only did Jesus suffer for us but that this is also true of the Father and of the Holy Spirit.

Jesus experienced vicariously the sins of the human race. He died an agonizing death as our substitute. As an extension of this we must accept that the Father and the Holy Spirit felt the pains of our sins vicariously also. In addition they suffered all the agony of the crucifixion experienced by Jesus. I don't pretend to understand how this took place, but if the Trinity teaching is correct it must have been so. I humbly thank Them with all my heart for doing this for me. Will you join me in this?

Please don't take this matter lightly. How well have you studied the material in this book? If you have just read it through you need to go back over it exploring the details so that you can file the truths outlined in the file marked 'What I believe' in your mental filing system. Please pray for the power of the Holy Spirit to help you as you meditate on this most difficult subject. It is difficult; but the rewards are enormous as you come to understand more fully the truth about the God we love and worship. I well remember the experience I had when, forced by the compelling power of the truths found in the Word of God, I accepted that Jesus is my Lord and my God. I was walking in the bush in Western Australia in the springtime and all the beautiful wildflowers of 'the Wildflower State' were in full bloom. After I had made my decision I felt so close to Jesus. I had never felt as close before and it seemed as though I was walking about four feet off the ground as I wended my way home. I still carry that same experience with me today as I think of the wonder of a God who loved me enough to give up everything and come and die for me.

When I accepted that the Holy Spirit is the third member of the Trinity I did not experience quite the same sensations. I guess it was because the breakthrough was not of the same magnitude, but I have rejoiced in the presence of my Holy Spirit friend as we walk together day by day. I certainly need Him in my life because I am a very ordinary human being and I desperately need God's guidance, encouragement and support every moment of every day. I glory in the fact that the Holy Spirit loves me sufficiently to nurse me along. I love Him for His wonderful goodness.

So, today, I am a committed Trinitarian. I praise the Heavenly Three for their love and for the privilege I have had in serving them in the ministry these many years. In retirement (Is there such a thing for a Christian?) I have stood in for some ministers while they were on leave, and for two years I taught Bible subjects at Avondale College, New South Wales, until, in 2000 I decided to concentrate on this book. My prayer is that it will bring glory to the Triune God I love and clarity of understanding to those of my readers who are interested in a greater comprehension of Bible truth.

We unreservedly confess that we do not understand all about God; however, the words of Isaac Watts admirably express what we do know and I close with them:

Almighty God to Thee
Be endless honours done,
The undivided Three,
And the mysterious One;
Where reason fails with all her powers,
There faith prevails, and love adores.